Whole Language Approach

Internet-Aided English Learning 2

Snap Shots of Heroes of Our Mind

이봉형 지음

영어감수 Bryn Elizabeth Keating

Shinasa

Snap Shots of Heroes of Our Mind

CONTENTS

일러두기

이 책은 영어의 읽기, 쓰기, 듣기, 말하기 능력을 전체적으로 향상시키기 위한 교재로 개발하였다. 수록된 내용은 인터넷 www.youtube.com이나 www.americanrhetoric.com에 올라 있는 동영상들이다. 동영상 14개 중 연설문을 비롯한 5개는 인터넷상의 자료를 활용하여 편집한 것이며 나머지 9개는 저자가 받아 적은 후 원어민의 감수를 받은 것이다. 일부는 소음이 심하여 원어민도 확신하기 어려운 부분이 몇 군데 있었다. 물음표로 표시해 두었다. 구태여 이러한 대사를 교재로 넣은 이유가 있다. 교실에서 배우는 것으로 끝나는 영어학습의 병폐를 덜기 위해 실제 현장의 영어를 경험시키기 위한 것이다. 강훈련을 하고 나면 실전은 한결 수월해 질 것이기 때문이다.

이 책은 대학 강의실 교재로 사용하기 위한 것이다. 따라서 본문을 한국어로 번역하는 일은 삼가 하였다. 한국어가 옆에 병기된 경우 학습자가 부지불식간에 한국어에 눈길이 가 공부가 될 리 없기 때문이다. 구성은 다음과 같다.

첫째 <To Help Out> 난에 <Key Words> and <Expressions>, <Proverbs Related to the Topic> 등을 두어 예습과 복습을 통해 본문 이해와 어휘, 표현 학습을 할 수 있도록 하였다. 반드시 어려운 표현이 아니더라도 학습효과를 위해 넣은 경우도 있다. 말은 알고 있는 것으로 끝나서는 안 되고 현장에서 써먹을 수 있어야 하기 때문에 어렴풋하게 알 것이 아니라 확실하게 알아둘 필요가 있다. <Listen and Fill in the Blanks> 난은 말할 것도 없이 청취력 향상을 위한 것이지만 cloze test의 괄호가 다른 교재와 다르다. 학습자가 주로 메워야 하는 공백은 주로 문장의 골격을 갖추는데 쓰이는 단어인 전치사, 조동사, 대명사 등이다. 문장의 내용전달에 크게 기여하지 못하는 단어이기 때문에 학습자에 따라 의아스럽게 생각할 수 있다. 그러나 이러한 구성은 분명한 의도가 있다. 발음 설명에서 반복하여 언급하고 있는 것처럼 영어발음의 관건은 영어의 리듬을 살리는 것이다. 이 때 강세가 매우 중요한 역할을 한다. 그러나 앞서 언급한 단어들은 단어 고유의 강세를 부여 받지 못하는 것들이다. 강세가 없다는 것은 곧 단어의 발음상 축소를 의미하므로 외국어 학습자에게 잘 들릴 리가 없다. 따라서 이러한 애매모호한 부분을 청취하는 훈련은 영어학습에서 문장의 의미를 파악하는데 매우 중요한 과정 중의 하나이다.

본 교재의 또 한 가지 특징은 <Pronunciation Bites: 한국인의 영어발음 오류유형> 난에서 영어의 청취, 말하기 능력향상을 위해 한국인들이 흔히 범하는 영어 발음 오류유형을 14가지로 분류하여 무엇이 문제인가를 설명한 다음 연습을 할 수 있는 기회를 제공한다는 점이다. 한국인의 입장에서 발음을 훈련한다는 점에서 효율성이 있을 것으로 기대된다. 맹목적인 반복훈련이 아닌 원인부터 파악한 후의 발음연습이라는 점에서 특징이 있다.

<Try it in English> 난은 본문에 나온 표현을 중심으로 자신이 직접 써 보면서 표현을 익혀 영작문에 대한 두려움을 떨쳐버리게 하는 데 목적이 있다. 의외로 많은 학생

들이 영어로 문장쓰기 자체에 두려움을 가지고 있다. 천리 길도 한 걸음부터라는 생각을 가지고 쉬운 것부터, 작은 것부터 일궈 나가자.

언어훈련은 말 만의 문제가 아니라는 점은 소위 Whole Language Approach의 방법론으로 정립되어 critical thinking abilities의 중요성이 강조되고 있다. 본 교재는 이러한 취지를 수용하여 <For Improvement of Your Critical Thinking>난을 두어 본문의 내용과 연계된 질문을 매 단원마다 하나씩 던져 자신의 의사를 개진하는 기회를 제공하고 있다. 이 항목은 학습자에게 과제로 내어 영어로 자신의 생각을 전개하는 훈련용으로 쓸 수 있다.

본 교재는 영어 일색으로 구성하지 않았다. 질문, 설명 등을 모두 영어로만 했을 경우 친학습자적 인상을 주지 못한다는 생각 하에 발음에 대한 설명이나 일부 질문을 한국어로 하였다.

마지막으로 본 교재에서 이용하고 있는 인터넷 동영상들은 내려받기가 불가능한 것들이다. 각 site에 접근하여 일회적 이용만 가능할 따름이다. 교재의 각 단원 제목 하단에 각 website들의 주소를 적어 놓았다. 내용을 볼 때마다 해당 파일을 내려받기를 하는 번거로움을 감수할 수밖에 없다.

영어단어 정의는 http://dictionary.reference.com/을 참고한 것이며 번거로움을 피하기 위해 본문에 별도의 인용표시를 생략하였다.

한 가지 아쉬운 점은 교재의 내용에 영화와 뉴스가 빠진 것이다. 본래는 뉴스와 영화를 중심으로 교재를 꾸며보려 했으나 CNN을 비롯한 뉴스와 영화의 지적재산권 정책이 너무나 엄격하여 결국 이들을 제외할 수밖에 없었다는 것이다.

아무쪼록 본 교재를 이용하는 모든 학습자들의 영어능력이 괄목상대, 일취월장하기를 기대한다.

2010년 봄 저자 이봉형

1 Remarks as Delivered
by Dr. Jim Yong Kim

March 2, 2009

from http://www.dartmouth.edu/

President Jim Yong Kim, President, Dartmouth College

http://www.dartmouth.edu/presidentelect/announcement-video.html

Thank you, Ed and Al, for your too generous introduction — and for the honor that you and your colleagues on the board of trustees have bestowed on me, in entrusting to me leadership of this magnificent institution — this college on the hill. And thank you, everyone, for the warmth you've already shown me as the newest member of the Dartmouth family.

On a personal note, I'd like to thank my parents. My father, Nhak Hee Kim who passed away more than twenty years ago, was a dentist — and dentists are among the most practical people on earth. He taught me the value of hard work, determination, and keeping both feet firmly on the ground. My mother, Oaksook Kim, studied theology and received her Ph.D. in philosophy. She taught me to respect every individual-while daring great things. Dare great things, keep both your feet on the ground. I hope that will prove to be a good formula for a president of Dartmouth.

As I embark on this exciting journey, I'm humbled by the example set by those who've gone before me — men like Ernest Hopkins, John Kemeny and John Sloan Dickey, about whom I will speak in a moment. And men like David McLaughlin and James Freedman - and of course Jim Wright.

Jim, you've devoted your life to Dartmouth, including 11 years as President. You leave enormous shoes to fill. Your tenure has enriched academic life at Dartmouth with an expansion of the faculty and the launch of new academic initiatives, and it's transformed the campus with an array of beautiful buildings. You and Susan created a warm and inviting atmosphere for all Dartmouth students, faculty and alums — and even for newcomers like me. My wife Younsook and I will do our best to continue to nurture this wonderful environment.

Younsook is sorry she can't be here today. As Ed mentioned, my second son was born just three days ago. It's been quite a week! My older son Thomas said to me just yesterday, "Daddy, why does everything have to happen to us at the same time?" But I can assure you that Thomas and Younsook are just as excited as I am in joining the Dartmouth community.

As I drove onto our snow covered campus today, I was struck once again by the spectacular setting in which Dartmouth students live and learn. I can't imagine a more beautiful place to be a student — or, for that matter, a College President.

But far beyond its physical beauty, Dartmouth is an institution without parallel — unique, even — in higher education. This is a community bound by rich traditions and a vibrant, ever-evolving culture. The diversity here is real yet there's a strong, abiding sense of family that extends out to our 69,000 alumni. As an anthropologist, I understand and value the importance of cherished traditions, a deeply shared campus culture and a diverse, yet cohesive community. My family and I are anxious to learn about and embrace every bit of it.

Indeed, I'm looking forward to working with all of you in the years to come to preserve and strengthen what makes Dartmouth so special . . . to ensure that our College is appreciated and its influence felt ever more widely in the world . . . and to secure its future in a rapidly changing global landscape. These will be my top priorities as President and Chief Advocacy Officer of Dartmouth College.

Young people from many, many backgrounds come here because of the exceptional learning experience that Dartmouth offers — whether as undergraduates or to join the first-rate professional schools and graduate programs that the College can point to with great pride.

Certainly, a vital part of that learning takes place in the classrooms in Kemeny, in Dartmouth Hall, the labs in Fairchild and among the stacks in Baker. But just as important to that learning is what happens out on Whitey Burnham Field, up on Mount Moosilauke, here on the stage in the Hop and, yes, even late at night on Webster Avenue. Education is not just about transferring knowledge — it is about learning how to be citizens of the world, how to work effectively with others as part of a team, and how to emerge from your studies with an enduring and robust philosophy of life.

Dartmouth is better equipped, perhaps more so than any other school in the nation, to teach these virtues . . . to help educate well-rounded leaders who can go forth and make the world a better place.

That brings me back to John Sloan Dickey, whose example and achievements were such an inspiration to me during the course of my selection as President of Dartmouth.

President Dickey left a lasting mark. He spent most of his career before becoming President outside of academia, but he believed passionately in the power of education to foster positive change. He was fond of telling students "the world's troubles are your troubles." And he believed that a Dartmouth education should equip young people to do something about those troubles. I believe that remains Dartmouth's most important mission today.

Like President Dickey, I've spent much of my career in places that are very different from Hanover. I've spent plenty of time in the classroom, but also in the slums of Peru, amid the rural poverty of Haiti, in post-genocidal Rwanda, and in the snowy cold of Siberia.

In my small way, I've tried to make the world's troubles my troubles. I've tackled them directly by setting up treatment programs, working to lower the prices of life-saving drugs and changing global health policy. But I've always known that my own impact as an individual will be limited. That's why I've worked to teach and mentor young people who can have a far greater impact than me. That's what attracted me to this extraordinary place called Dartmouth College. Here, we have all the tools to prepare an army of future leaders: students like you who will go out into the world and, by making the most of what you learn from your professors and from each other, make that world more productive, more enlightened, more humane and more just.

We know we can create these leaders because Dartmouth faculty do what is thought to be impossible at other institutions — you teach so well that students give the quality of your instruction a 97 percent approval rating. At the same time, you do ground-breaking research and make great contributions to your field. It will be my job to ensure that you, the faculty, reach your highest aspirations, both as teachers and as scholars.

We know Dartmouth graduates can change the world . . . they already are. From the last two Secretaries of the Treasury, Henry Paulson and Timothy Geithner, to the Ochieng brothers, Milton and Fred. Inspired by a Dartmouth community service trip to Nicaragua, the Ochiengs returned to the small village in rural Kenya where they were born to start a clinic. This clinic administers not just medical care but hope itself. Dartmouth graduates all over the world are doing great things, and making us all proud.

I've found again and again in my career that when you set bold, ambitious goals, plenty of people will tell you that you're crazy or that it just can't be done. That's what they told us at Partners In Health, when we wanted to treat people suffering from multi-drug-resistant tuberculosis in the slums of Lima, Peru. And it's what they told us at the World Health Organization when we wanted to treat three million people living with HIV in developing countries.

I'm happy to say that we didn't listen to the naysayers. Now, people across the globe *are* being treated for both drug-resistant tuberculosis and HIV, and the naysayers have been converted.

If we teach nothing else at Dartmouth, we must teach our students to find their passion, to aim high, work hard, and settle for nothing less than to transform the world. I know Dartmouth students can achieve anything to which they commit themselves.

My job will be to make sure that Dartmouth gives you, our students, all the tools you need to do unprecedented things — whether in science or the arts or business or health — things that even today seem unimaginable. Who could ask for a better job than that?

The anthropologist Margaret Mead once said, "Never underestimate the capacity of a small group of committed souls to change the world, indeed, it's the only thing that ever has." Well, we're not such a small group at Dartmouth and I've already met a lot of committed souls here. The greatest privilege of my life will be to work with all of you as President, to make the world's troubles our troubles, and to train leaders the likes of which the world has never seen, to take them on.

Thank you all for welcoming me. I can't wait to get started. It is, as we all know, a small college. And yet the Kim family already loves it. Thank you very much.

Words and Expressions Check-Up

board of trustees *noun* a group of persons, appointed to administer the affairs of a company or institution.

initiative *noun* an introductory act or step, leading action: *to take the initiative in making friends.*

abiding *adjective* continuing, enduring: *an abiding belief.*

cohesive *adjective* cohering, tending to cohere: *a cohesive organization.*

appreciate *verb* to value, regard highly or place a high estimate on: *to appreciate good coffee.*

academia *noun* the milieu of a university or academy, academe.

genocide *noun* the intentional and systematic extermination of a racial group. an army of determiner any group of persons organized for any purpose.

naysayer *noun* a person who habitually expresses negative or pessimistic views.

tuberculosis *noun* a disease that affects the lungs.

pass away *phrasal verb* to die: *He passed away during the night.*

keep one's feet on the ground *idiom Your intelligence helps you to keep your feet on the ground.*

well-rounded *adjective* having desirably varied abilities or attainments.

bring back *phrasal verb* to remind of: *I was brought back to the present once again.*

last *verb* to go on or continue: *The conference lasted three weeks.*

foster *verb* to promote the growth: *to foster new ideas.*

administer *verb* to bring into use or operation.

HIV=human immunodeficiency virus.

multi-drug resistant tuberculosis (MDR-TB) a TB that is resistant at least to isoniazid (INH) and rifampicin (RMP), the two most powerful first-line anti-TB drugs.

convert *verb* to note a specified type of person who has been converted from the religion or attitudes: *a converted Muslim, a converted criminal.*

commit oneself to something *phrasal verb* to bind by pledge or assurance.

arts *noun* (*used with a singular verb*) the humanities: *a college of liberal arts.*

committed soul *noun There are a few committed souls who work tirelessly for the common cause.*

Proverbs Related to the Text

- As you sow, so you reap.
- The tongue is sharper than the sword.
- Nothing ventured, nothing gained.
- A half the world knows not how the other half lives.

Listen and Fill in the Blanks.

As I drove onto our snow __________ campus today, I was struck once again by the spectacular _________ in which Dartmouth students live and learn. I can't imagine a more beautiful place to be a student — or, for that matter, a College President.

But far beyond its ____________ beauty, Dartmouth is an institution ___________ _____________ – unique, even – in higher education. This is a community bound by rich traditions and a vibrant, ________-evolving culture. The diversity here is real yet there's a strong, abiding sense of family that _______ ________ to our 69,000 alumni. As an anthropologist, I understand and value the importance of cherished traditions, a deeply shared campus culture and a diverse, yet ___________ community. My family and I are anxious to learn about and embrace every ______ _____ _____.

Indeed, I'm looking forward to _________ _______ all of you in the years to come to preserve and strengthen what makes Dartmouth so special . . . to ensure that our College is appreciated and its influence felt ever more widely in the world . . . and to secure its future in a rapidly changing global ___________. These will be my top priorities as President and Chief Advocacy Officer of Dartmouth College.

Pronunciation Bites

한국인 영어발음오류유형1 : [z, ʒ, ʤ]의 구분

영어의 Jesus의 첫 자음과 두 번째 자음은 한국인들에 같은 소리로 들린다. 둘 다 한국어의 [ㅈ]으로 인식된다. 마찬가지로 jazz의 첫 소리와 마지막 소리도 같은 [ㅈ]으로 들려온다. Judge의 경우는 어떤가? 첫 소리와 끝소리가 같은 [ㅈ]으로 들린다. 또한 가지, measure 등의 철자 < s >는 어떻게 실현되나? 음성기호로 이들 단어의 영어 발음을 표기해 보자.

Jesus [ʤizəs]

jazz [ʤæz]

judge [ʤʌʤ]

measure [mɛʒər]

위 음성기호 표기에서 알 수 있듯이 우리 귀에 [ㅈ]으로 들리는 자음은 실제 영어에서는 세 가지로 별개의 소리임을 알 수 있다. 첫째는 잇몸마찰음 [z]가 있고 두 번째는 경구개 마찰음 [ʒ], 세 번째가 폐찰음 [ʤ]인 것이다. 마찰음은 혀끝이나 혀날이 입천장에 닿지 않도록 해야 하며 폐찰음은 닿아야 한다. 이 세 가지 소리 구분에 주의하면서 다음을 발음해 보자.

Pronunciation Excercise

a. [z] zeal, zinc, fuzzy, razor, lose, eyes, pens, falls

b. [ʒ] Asia, vision, allusion, conclusion, occasion, division

c. [ʤ] gem, magic, juice, major, enjoy, pigeon, imagine, lodge, badge

Try it in English

1. 금년은 그 과학자가 작고한 지 100주년이 된다.

   This year __________a centennial since the scientist __________ _________.

2. 그 사람은 큰일을 할 사람이다.

   He is a man to __________ ____________ ____________.

For Improvement of Your Critical Thinking

Question: President Kim was selected as the new President of Dartmouth College, one of the most prestige universities in the US. When he was announced as the new president, the student association of Dartmouth was not happy about the decision and virtually disavowed him. The foremost reason of the rejection was that he is from an Asian country. Later on they revoked their stance, but it inevitably reveals the deeply rooted racism in the white dominated community. If you were President Kim, how would you react to the students' imprudent behavior?

Dartmouth College

Dartmouth College (pronounced /ˈdɑrtməθ/) is a private, coeducational university located in Hanover, New Hampshire. Incorporated as "Trustees of Dartmouth College," it is a member of the Ivy League and one of the nine Colonial Colleges founded before the American Revolution. In addition to its undergraduate liberal arts program, Dartmouth has medical, engineering, and business schools, as well as 19 graduate programs in the arts and sciences. With a total enrollment of 5,848, Dartmouth is the smallest school in the Ivy League.

Established in 1769 by Congregational minister Eleazar Wheelock with funds largely raised by the efforts of Native American preacher Samson Occom, the College's initial mission was to acculturate and Christianize the Native Americans. After a long period of financial and political struggles, Dartmouth emerged from relative obscurity in the early twentieth century. In 2004, Booz Allen Hamilton selected Dartmouth College as a model of institutional endurance "whose record of endurance has had implications and benefits for all American organizations, both academic and commercial," citing *Trustees of Dartmouth College v. Woodward* and Dartmouth's successful self-reinvention in the late 1800s. Dartmouth alumni, from Daniel Webster to the many donors in the nineteenth and twentieth centuries, have been famously involved in their college.

Dartmouth is located on a rural 269-acre (1.1 km^2) campus in the Upper Valley region of New Hampshire. Given the College's isolated location, participation in athletics and the school's Greek system is high. Dartmouth's 34 varsity sports teams compete in the Ivy League conference of the NCAA Division I. Students are also well-known for preserving a variety of strong campus traditions.

President Kim talks with parents and students during Sophomore Family Weekend (photo by Joseph Mehling '69) (http://www.dartmouth.edu).

http://www.wikipedia.org

2 The Simpsons
No Pets in Heaven

http://www.youtube.com/watch?v=6xbuFLFfD4k&feature=related

Clockwise from top left: Marge, Homer, Bart, Santa's Little Helper (dog), Snowball II (cat), Lisa, and Maggie in the center.

Will my dog Pepper be there?

I'm sorry. But the answer is no.

Why not?

Because heaven is for people.

What about my cat Snowball?

I'm sorry but the answer is no.

Will there be cavemen in heaven?

Certainly not.

Ah, ma'am. Ah, ma'am?

What if you're a really good person, but you're in a really really bad fight, and your leg gets gangrene, and it has to be amputated, will it be waiting for you in heaven?

For the last time, Bart, yes.

Key Words & Expressions

gangrene *noun* death of soft tissue due to obstructed circulation.

caveman *noun* A prehistoric or primitive human beings living in caves.

amputate *verb* to cut off all or part of a limb or digit of the body: *Because of space limitations the editor amputated the latter part of the article.*

heaven *noun* the abode of God, the angels, and the spirits of the righteous after death.

Proverbs Related to the Text

- Every man is a fool sometimes and none at all times.
- Every cloud has a silver lining.

Listen and Fill in the Blanks.

Will my dog Pepper be there?

I'm sorry. But the answer is no.

Why not?

Because heaven ______ _________ people.

What about my cat Snowball?

I'm sorry but the answer is no.

________ _________ ________ cavemen in heaven?

Certainly not.

Ah, ma'am. Ah, ma'am? What if you're a really good person, but _________ ______ _______ really really bad fight, and your leg _______ gangrene, and it has to be ____________, will it be waiting for you in heaven?

For the last time, Bart, yes.

Pronunciation Bites

한국인 영어발음오류유형 2 : 축소모음

오류유형 11에서 한국어의 리듬은 음절수에 의존하는 반면 영어는 강세 수에 의존한다는 점을 살펴보고 연습해 볼 것이다. 그렇다면 리듬이란 '일정한 길이의 단위가 반복되는 현상'을 의미하는데 음절수에 관계없이 강세에 의존하여 리듬단위의 길이를 일정하게 유지하는 등시성(isochrony)를 어떻게 유지할 수 있나? 그것은 '강세 의존 리듬'을 가진 언어의 특이한 현상 때문에 가능하다. 비밀은 축소모음 (schwa)에 있다. 다시 말해서 문장 상에서 강세를 받지 못한 음절은 모음의 길이와 음향적 특성이 축소되고 자음이 탈락하는 방편을 취한다. 그러면 해당 음절의 길이가 줄어들어 시간의 단축을 가져오게 된다. 그렇다면 어떤 단어가 축소의 대상이 되나? 그것은 명사, 동사, 형용사, 부사 등의 소위 내용어(content word)에 속하지 않은 나머지 기능어(function word) 단어들로서 관사, 전치사, 접속사, 조동사, 대명사 (의문, 지시대명사 제외) 등이 여기에 속한다. 다음을 보자.

(Which is the)$_1$ (train to)$_2$ (Daejeon)$_3$ (please)$_4$?

리듬의 단위 1에서 which를 제외한 is, the 리듬의 단어 2에서 to 단위 3에서 두 번째 음절 jeon은 강세가 없는 음절로서 모음이 schwa [ə]로 발음된다. 이 발음은 영어모음 중에서 빈도수가 가장 높아 일상적인 대화에서 모유의 1/4 가량이 이 축소모음인 것으로 알려져 있다. 따라서 영어모음 발음에서 축소모음의 발음을 제대로 하는 가는 앞의 리듬의 문제와 함께 매우 중요하다. 축소모음의 조음은 다음과 같다. 혀의 위치는 입안의 중간위치에 놓되 모음의 길이, 크기는 최소화한다. 축소모음은 영어에서 강세가 없는 음절의 80%이상이라고 보면 틀림없다. 철자를 의식한 한국인의 영어발음에서 큰 특징 중의 하나가 축소모음을 제대로 내지 못한다는 점이다. 다음의 경우를 연습해 보자.

Pronunciation Excercise

<i> possible, conflict, victim, happily, luckily

<e> gentlemen, effect, except, raises, grosses, Sweden

<a> woman, about, affect, accept, and, alone

<o> oblige, razor, for, decorative, doctor

<u> suppose, picture, figure, failure

Try it in English

1. 3 + 4는 얼마인가?

   How ______ is three ________ four?

2. 9 x 8은 얼마인가?

   How ________ is nine __________ eight?

3. 이 영화는 흥행에 크게 성공했다.

   The film got a big ______-_______ success.

For Improvement of Your Critical Thinking

Question: Animation movies or television sitcoms are often a lot of fun, aren't they? Sometimes they make us happy. The flip side, however, is that they more often than not contain violence or obscenities that may have a bad influence on adolescents. Are you for or against animation movies or TV series? Present your ideas.

The Simpsons, an American Sitcom

The Simpsons is an American animated television sitcom created by Matt Groening for the Fox Broadcasting Company. The series is a satirical parody of a middle class American lifestyle epitomized by its eponymous family, which consists of Homer, Marge, Bart, Lisa, and Maggie. The show is set in the fictional city of Springfield, and lampoons American culture, society and television, and many aspects of the human condition.

The family was conceived by Groening shortly before a pitch for a series of animated shorts with the producer James L. Brooks. Groening created a dysfunctional family and named the characters after members of his own family, substituting Bart for his own name. The shorts became a part of The *Tracey Ullman Show* on April 19, 1987. After a three-season run, the sketch was developed into a half-hour prime time show and was an early hit for Fox, becoming the first Fox series to land in the Top 30 ratings in a season (1989~990).

Since its debut on December 17, 1989 the show has broadcast 441 episodes and the twentieth season began airing on September 28, 2008. *The Simpsons Movie,* a feature-length film, was released in theaters worldwide on July 26 and July 27, 2007, and grossed US$527 million worldwide.

The Simpsons has won dozens of awards since it debuted as a series, including 24 Primetime Emmy Awards, 26 Annie Awards and a Peabody Award. *Time* magazine's December 31, 1999 issue named it the 20th century's best television series, and on January 14, 2000 the Simpson family was awarded a star on the Hollywood Walk of Fame. The Simpsons is the longest-running American sitcom, the longest-running American animated program, and in 2009 it surpassed *Gunsmoke* as the longest running American primetime entertainment series. Homer's annoyed grunt "D'oh!" has been adopted into the English lexicon, while The Simpsons has influenced many adult-oriented animated sitcoms.

http://www.wikipedia.org

3 Phishing Scams in Plain English

http://www.youtube.com/watch?v=sqRZGhiHGxg&fwature=fvw

TrustedBank™

Dear valued customer of TrustedBank,

We have recieved notice that you have recently attempted to withdraw the following amount from your checking account while in another country: $135.25.

If this information is not correct, someone unknown may have access to your account. As a safety measure, please visit our website via the link below to verify your personal information:

http://www.trustedbank.com/general/custverifyinfo.asp

Once you have done this, our fraud department will work to resolve this discrepency. We are happy you have chosen us to do business with.

Thank you,
TrustedBank

Member FDIC © 2005 TrustedBank, Inc.

An example of a phishing e-mail, disguised as an official e-mail from a (fictional) bank. The sender is attempting to trick the recipient into revealing confidential information by "confirming" it at the *phisher's* website. Note the misspelling of the words *received* and *discrepancy*. Such mistakes are common in most phishing e-mails. Also note that although the URL of the bank's webpage appears to be legitimate, it actually links to the *phisher's* webpage.
(http://www.google.co.kr/imglanding?imgurl)

You've probably seen it. You receive an e-mail from your bank or trusted company, and it's asking you for information. It looks real, but it's designed to fool you into handing over important information. This is a scam called Phishing, and you need to avoid it. This is Phishing Scams in Plain English.

Most of us have gotten used to doing business on-line. We buy and sell things. We have accounts with sensitive information. The risk of doing business on-line is low as long as you deal directly with organizations you trust. Problems occur when criminals impersonate these organizations and fool you into handing over sensitive information like account numbers, passwords, and PIN numbers.

The key to avoiding this scam is awareness. Here's one example. You receive an e-mail that looks like a trustworthy message from a bank. It asks you to click a link to verify information. You assume it's legit, so you click the link and log onto what appears to be your bank's website. At this point, the scam is complete.

You've handed over your bank password to the crooks, who can use it to take your money. They were able to fool you by impersonating the bank's website. There are a few keys to detecting Phishing e-mails. They often try to scare you by saying your account has been accessed or security has been compromised.

They also insist that you to click a link to verify information or fill out a form. Do not click links or fill out forms in suspicious e-mails. The e-mail may also have misspellings, and call you something like "Valued Customer." The crooks don't know your name.

Remember Phishing e-mails may use the exact same logos, phone numbers and addresses that appear on your statements or bills.

Always be suspicious of an e-mail that asks for your information. No exceptions! If you receive Phishing e-mail, stay calm. There is no risk to receiving it; just delete it. You can also safely report it by forwarding it to: reportphishing@antiphishing.org or spam@uce.gov.

If an e-mail does lead you to a suspicious website, remember to look at the web address. The address in you browse should look familiar. If you suspect that criminals have your information, immediately contact organizations where you have accounts. To protect yourself in the long run, you might also consider anti-Phishing software. Further, check your on-line accounts and credit reports regularly, and quickly report anything that is out of place.

Phishing scams are a growing threat on the Internet. By being aware of the scam, you can feel confident in working with companies on-line. Yea!

I am Lee LeFever, and this has been Phishing Scams in Plain English on the Commoncraft Show. One more thing: You can download presentation quality versions of our videos without ads like this in the Commoncraft Store.

Key Words & Expressions

Impersonate *verb* to assume the character or appearance of someone: *He was arrested for impersonating a celebrity.*

fool *verb* to trick or deceive: *They wanted to fool him.*

compromise *verb* to expose or make vulnerable to danger: *a military negligence compromised the nation's defenses.*

crook *noun* a dishonest person, a sharper, a swindler.

verify *verb* to prove the truth of, confirm.

forward *verb* to send forward, transmit to a new address: *to forward the mail.*

browse *verb* to look through or glance at casually: *They are browsing the websites for something to read.*

Proverbs Related to the Text

- What youth is used to, age remembers.
- Young men are fitter to invent than to judge, fitter for execution than for counsel, fitter for new projects than for settled business.
- Easy come easy go.
- He that will not endure labor in this world let him not be born.

Listen and Fill in the Blanks.

You've probably seen it. You receive an e-mail from your bank or trusted company, and it's asking you for information. It looks real, but it's _________ to __________ you into handing over important information. This is a scam called Phishing, and you need to avoid it. This is Phishing Scams in Plain English.

Most of us have gotten used to doing business on-line. We buy and sell things. We have accounts with sensitive information. The risk of doing business on-line is low as long as you deal directly with organizations you trust. Problems occur when criminals __________ these organizations and fool you into handing over sensitive information like account numbers, passwords, and ______ numbers.

The key to avoiding this scam is __________. Here's one example. You receive an e-mail that looks like a __________ message from a bank. It asks you to click a link to verify information. You assume it's _________, so you click the link and log onto what appears to be your bank's website. At this point, the scam is complete.

You've handed over your bank password to the crooks, who can use it to take your money. They were able to fool you by __________ the bank's website. There are a few keys to detecting Phishing e-mails. They often try to scare you by saying your account has been ___________ or security has been ___________.

Pronunciation Bites

한국인 영어발음오류유형 3 : 비음화

한국어의 소리현상을 영어에 전이하여 생기는 오류도 무시할 수 없다. 한국어에는 독립문 /toklipmun/ → 동님문 [tonimmun], 직면 /tsikmyən/ → 징면 [tsiŋmyən]에서 보는 바와 같이 콧소리 자음 /m, n, ŋ/ 앞의 자음이 콧소리가 되는 경향이 있다. 이런 비음화를 영어를 할 때도 적용하는 것을 흔히 본다. 다음의 경우이다.

Whitman /witmən/ → [witʰɨman] 또는 [winman]
Beckman /bekmən/ → [bekʰɨman] 또는 [beŋman]
Big Mac /big mæk/ → [bigɨmæk] 또는 [biŋmæk]
batman /bætmən/ → [bætʰɨmæn] 또는 [bænmæn]
gate number /geit nʌmbər/ → [geitʰɨnʌmbər] 또는 [geinnʌmbər]

다음의 경우도 '꽃잎' /k'ots ip/ → 꼰닙 [k'onnip]에서 /ㄴ/-삽입과 비음화가 동시에 일어나는 현상을 적용하여 영어를 할 때도 다음과 같이 나타나고 있다.

what you want → [wannju wəntʰɨ]
What you need → [wannju nidɨ]

영어에는 이런 /ㄴ/-삽입이나 비음화/현상이 존재하지 않는다. 비음화를 시키지 않도록 주의해야 한다. 비음화처럼 정도는 심하지 않으나 /ㄹ/ 앞에서 /ㄴ/이 /ㄹ/로 바뀌는 예컨대 환란 → 활란, 신라 → 실라 와 같은 현상을 영어에 적용한 다음의 경우도 있다.

only → [oulli]

unless → [əllesɨ]

한국어에서는 모음 '이' 앞에서 잇소리 /ㅅ, ㄷ, ㅌ, ㄴ, ㄹ/의 조음점이 후퇴하는 구개음화현상이 일어난다. 영어를 할 때 특히 모음 /i/ 앞에서 /s/를 /ʃ/로 발음하는 현상은 한국어의 영향이다.

missing → [miʃiŋ]

miss it → [miʃit]

see, C, sea → [ʃi]

그 밖에 queen, quiz, question에서의 [kw] 연쇄를 한국어와 같은 요령으로 하지 않도록 주의해야 한다. 위의 단어나 구절을 한국어의 소리현상을 적용하지 않도록 주의하면서 발음해 보자.

Pronunciation Excercise

Big Mac, gate number, Whitman, catnip, outline, outlet

sea, missing, passing, C, seesaw, cease

queen, question, quiz, quilt, quick, query, quell

Try it in English

1. 스팸메일은 누가 퍼뜨리나?

   Who _______ to __________ spam mail.

2. 요즘 악성코드가 침투한 컴퓨터가 많다.

   Recently it is common to find a computer _________ by ________ ________

3. 전화사기범이 검거 되었다.

   The _______ ________ criminal was arrested.

For Improvement of Your Critical Thinking

Question: During the past centuries, we have been thrilled by the benefits stemming from the revolutionary technology created by our ancestors. It is true that they have made a significant difference in our daily life. Yet, unfortunately, modern technology casts a dark shadow in another way. With computers, fraud by e-mail, spam e-mails and hacking represent the negative side effects of the scientific inventions. What do you think about the impact of modern technology on our everyday life?

Phishing

Logos of Anti-phishing organizations

In the field of computer security, phishing is the criminally fraudulent process of attempting to acquire sensitive information such as usernames, passwords and credit card details by masquerading as a trustworthy entity in an electronic communication. Communications purporting to be from popular social web sites, auction sites, on-line payment processors or IT administrators are commonly used to lure the unsuspecting public. Phishing is typically carried out by e-mail or instant messaging, and it often directs users to enter details at a fake website whose look and feel are almost identical to the legitimate one. Even when using server authentication, it may require tremendous skill to detect that the website is fake. Phishing is an example of social engineering techniques used to fool users, and exploits the poor usability of current web security technologies. Attempts to deal with the growing number of reported phishing incidents include legislation, user training, public awareness, and technical security measures.

A phishing technique was described in detail in 1987, and the first recorded use of the term "phishing" was made in 1996. The term is a variant of *fishing*, probably influenced by *phreaking*, and alludes to baits used to "catch" financial information and passwords.

www.wikipedia.org

4 Thomas Edison

http://www.youtube.com/watch?v=NqjJwyUXcd4

Thomas Edison's first successful light bulb model, used in public demonstration at Menlo Park, December 1879

Thomas Edison, a man considered to be the greatest inventor ever, started his career as a telegraph operator, and when he was little, he was very much interested in business.

Edison also established the first industrial lab in the world history. Edison invented many things in his lifetime and had over one thousand ninety three patents.

Before he died, Thomas Edison invented many improvements to the telegraph system and invented different telegraph systems. That got him enough money to make a new lab.

In 1948, Thomas Edison got the Medal of Honor for inventing the phonograph. Edison invented the phonograph, lithograph, Dictaphone, and improved film projectors, storage batteries, and of course, the light bulb. Edison made a new invention every 11 days and made a major invention every six months.

Many people believe that Thomas Edison invented the first light bulb. What Thomas Edison did invent was the first reusable light bulb but not the first light bulb

What Edison needed and did find was the right filament that would let the light bulb work in everyday use.

He found a material that would burn so hot that it would glow without burning out. When Thomas Edison was asked how many times it took him to make a successful light bulb, he said he found over 14,000 ways how not to make light bulb.

Late after the invention of the light bulb, Edison made the world's first power-plant that later lit up a New York City block. The power plant housed some of the first dynamos, switches, electric meters, fuses, distribution lines, and regulators.

Key Words & Expressions

phonograph *noun* sound-reproducing machine using records.

lithography *noun* the art or process of writing on a flat, specially prepared stone with some greasy or oily substance.

Dictaphone *noun* a trademark used for an apparatus that records and reproduces dictation for transcription.

distribution line *noun* transmission line and distribution line are sometimes used interchangeably, but a distribution line is normally considered to be a line that carries less than 69,000 volts and is used to distribute power drawn from high-voltage transmission systems to end-use customers. (http://www.wikipedia.org)

regulator *noun* a device for maintaining a designated characteristic at a predetermined value.

power plant *noun* a plant necessary for the generation of power as electric or nuclear power.

Proverbs Related to the Text

- Necessity is the mother of invention.
- God helps them that help themselves.
- Practice makes perfect.
- No sweet without some sweat.

Listen and Fill in the Blanks.

What Edison ____________ and did find was the right filament that ________ _______ the light bulb __________ in everyday use.

He found material that burn so hot that glow without burning out. When Thomas Edison was asked how many times _____ ________ ______ to make a successful ________ _________, he said he found over 14,000 ways how not to make light bulb.

Late after the invention of the light bulb, Edison made the world's first power-plant that later _______ _______ a New York City block. The power plant housed some of the first dynamos, switches, electric meters, ________, ______________ __________, and regulators.

Pronunciation Bites

한국인 영어발음오류유형 4 : 모음 [ɨ] 삽입

일본인들이 hot, cold, Mexico, McDonald's 등을 [하또], [코루도], [메끼시코], [마구도나루도]으로 발음하는 것을 보면 웃음이 절로 나온다. 마치 어떤 기계의 부품을 해체해 놓은 것처럼 영어의 음절을 엿가락처럼 늘려놓고 있다. 이유는 간단하다. 일본어의 음절구조는 특별한 경우를 제외하고 <자음-모음> 구조로 되어 있어 영어를 이 구조에 꿰어 맞추다 보니 이렇게 된 것이다. 모국어의 음절구조가 외국어발음에서 단단히 개입한다는 것을 확인할 수 있다. 그러나 이 문제는 한국인의 경우도 정도의 차이만 있을 따름이지 마찬가지로 나타나고 있다. 다음의 경우을 보자. 여기서 음성기호 [ɨ]는 한국어 [으]를 가리킨다.

a. strike /straik/ → [sit^{h}ɨra.i.k^{h}ɨ] 스트라이크
b. boat /bout/ → [pot^{h}ɨ] 보트
c. church /tʃʌtʃ/ → [tʃʌtʃi] 처치

strike의 경우는 1음절이 4절로 바뀌고 boat는 단어 끝에 [ɨ]를 삽입하고 church의

경우는 [i]를 삽입하고 있다. 원인은 (a)와 (c)의 경우는 한국어의 음절 구조는 자음-모음-자음 (CVC)의 구조와 음절말 7종성 (p, t, k, m, n, ŋ, l)아닌 경우 모음삽입을 통하여 한국어 구조에 순응하고 있다. 그러나 (b)의 경우는 음절만의 문제라면 한국어에서 음절종성으로 문제가 없음에도 모음이 삽입하고 있다. 이 경우는 또 다른 문제로서 폐쇄음 자음의 파열(release)의 문제로 보면 된다. 즉 한국어의 음절말 7개의 자음들은 파열이 일어나지 않는 상태에서 조음이 종료된다. 리듬의 면에서 모든 음절을 대등하게 다루는 리듬과 더불어 '종성 불파 현상'은 한국어 발음이 듣는 이에게 부드러운 인상을 주지 못하는 이유가 된다. 그런데 영어에서는 통계에 따르면 [ou]와 같은 이중모음이나 장모음 다음의 폐쇄음들은 흔히 파열을 하는 경향이 있는 것으로 조사되어 있다. 따라서 (b)의 모음삽입은 이러한 영어의 파열을 유지하기 위한 방편으로 볼 수 있다. 모음 앞의 모든 자음은 파열이 되기 때문이다. 이 점에 주의하여 다음을 연습해 보자.

Pronunciation Excercise

a. evening, patron, Whitman, batman, meatball

b. judge, budge, bridge, catch, dispatch, coach

c. seat, peak, bag, keep, beat, bead, seed

Try it in English

1. 송전선은 발전소와 우리 가정을 연결해 준다.

__________ __________ connect __________ _________ and our homes.

2. 전구는 우리 동네를 환하게 밝혀준다.

_________ ________ _________ _________ our neighborhood.

3. 공포영화가 요즘 유행하고 있다.

The ________ movies are _________ now.

For Improvement of Your Critical Thinking

Question: Obviously, our modern civilization owes much to the brilliant minds of inventors and adventurers. In contrast, scientific creations sometimes give rise to social or ethical problems in our society. Describe a bad function of a scientific creation in modern history.

Thomas Edison

Thomas Alva Edison (February 11, 1847~October 18, 1931) was an American inventor, scientist and businessman who developed many devices that greatly influenced life around the world, including the phonograph, the motion picture camera, and a long-lasting, practical electric light bulb. Dubbed "The Wizard of Menlo Park" by a newspaper reporter, he was one of the first inventors to apply the principles of mass production and large teamwork to the process of invention, and therefore is often credited with the creation of the first industrial research laboratory.

Edison is considered one of the most prolific inventors in history, holding 1,093 U.S. patents in his name, as well as many patents in the United Kingdom, France and Germany. He is credited with numerous inventions that contributed to mass communication and, in particular, telecommunications. His advanced work in these fields was an outgrowth of his early career as a telegraph operator. Edison originated the concept and implementation of electric-power generation and distribution to homes, businesses, and factories — a crucial development in the modern industrialized world. His first power plant was on Manhattan Island, New York.

Transcript *"Before starting experiments on the incandescent electric light system, many memorandums were drawn up as to a general system that would permit a subdivision of the light into small units analogous to gas jets and with commercial economy superior to the prevailing gas system. The thought was, if it was to be successful, all the units must be worked in multiply. This necessitated the creation of lamps of very high resistance to diminish the enormous investment in copper if necessary, if lower resistance lamps were to be used. (For the safety) This necessitated identifying hair-like filaments of high air-resistance material. On October twenty-first 1871, numerous experiments resulted in the production of a small unit lamp of comparatively enormous resistance. The filament being under conditions of great stability after this result, I knew the problem approached commercial solution. As these lamp experiments continued, other parts of the general system was actively experimented upon. The dynamo, as then invoked, was extremely inefficient; the loss approaching fifty percent due to some misunderstanding among electricians which I never comprehended. However, these experiments produced a dynamo of which ninety percent of the energy was useful. Then meters for measuring the current were used by thousands of customers and also a host of accessories like underground conduit, circuits, sockets, et cetera were necessary to make a complete system of distribution, all of which was accomplish..."*

http://commons.wikimedia.org/wiki/ File:Edison_speech,_1920s.ogg

5 Michael Jordan

http://www.youtube.com/watch?v=GPkCwz_gNGM&feature=fvst

Born in Brooklyn, New York, but raised in North Carolina, Michael Jordan played baseball, football, and basketball throughout high school.

Jordan under scholarship to the University of North Carolina, where he quickly proved his potential, becoming the Atlantic Coast Conference's Freshman of the Year. In that first season as a Tar Heel, Jordan helped, James Worthy lead the team into the NCAA finals against Patrick Ewing at the Georgetown Hoyas.

Jordan hit the shot in the final seconds to give North Carolina the sixty-three to sixty-two victory, and North Carolina its second division 1 championship. Jordan went on to describe this game-winning shot as the major turning point in his basketball career.

In his junior season, Jordan would win just about every trophy they could give away, receiving honors such as the USBWA College Player of the Year, the Naismith College Player of the Year, and the Adolph Rupp Trophy. However, without Worthy, Jordan and North Carolina would never win another NCAA title, advancing only as far as the Elite Eight and the Sweet Sixteen in the following years.

In 1984, Jordan would begin his legendary pro career with the Chicago Bulls, where he would go on to win six NBA championships.

Key Words & Expressions

Tar Heel *noun* the mascot of the University of North Carolina.

USBWA *noun* United States Basketball Writers Association.

Naismith College Player of the Year *noun* The Naismith College Player of the Year award, named for basketball inventor James Naismith, is given annually by the Atlanta Tipoff Club to college basketball's top male and female player. The first award was given to Lew Alcindor, now known as Kareem Abdul-Jabbar, in 1969. The first women's award was given in 1983. (http://www.wikipedia.org)

The Adolph Rupp Trophy *noun* The Adolph F. Rupp Trophy is an award given annually to the top player in men's Division I NCAA basketball, considered one of the top.

James Worthy *noun* James Ager Worthy (born February 27, 1961 in Gastonia, North Carolina), is a retired Hall of Fame American college and professional basketball player. Named as one of the 50 Greatest Players in NBA History, "Big Game James" was a seven time NBA All-Star and three time NBA champion. A standout for the North Carolina Tar Heels, the 6 ft 9 in (2.05 m) small forward was the MOP of the 1982 NCAA Tournament and #1 pick of the 1982 NBA Draft. (http://www.wikipedia.org)

NCAA National Collegiate Athletic Association.

Proverbs Related to the Text

- Variety is the spice of life.
- Live and let live.
- Better be the head of dog than the tail of a lion.
- Leave well enough alone

Listen and Fill in the Blanks.

In his junior season, Jordan would win just ___________ _________ trophy they could give away, receiving honors such as the USBWA College Player of the Year, the Naismith College Player of the Year, and the Adolph Rupp Trophy. However, without Worthy, Jordan and North Carolina would never win another _________ title, advancing only _____ _______ _____ the Elite Eight and the Sweet Sixteen in the following years.

In 1984, Jordan would begin his legendary pro career with the Chicago Bulls, where he ________ _______ _______ ______ win six NBA championships.

Pronunciation Bites

한국인 영어발음오류유형 5 : 철자 <o>

영어 철자 <o>를 한국어의 [오]에 대응시키려는 경향은 매우 강하다. 흔히 다음 단어의 모음을 모조리 [오]로 발음하여 아래 대화에서와 같은 의사소통의 장애가 오기도 한다.

A Korean Tourist : Excuse me! I'm looking for the Rosslin subway station. Could you show me where it is?

A Local: I have no idea. Could you say it again, please?

T: Rosslin [roslin] subway station.

L: You sound to mean Rosslin [ra:slin] subway station. It's over there.

T: Sorry to confuse you.

L: My pleasure.

영어의 모음기호는 실제로 다양한 소리를 가리키며 특히 철자 <o> 의 경우는 다음과 같이 6가지의 가능성이 있다. 모음의 경우 철자에 의존한 발음을 특히 경계해야 한다.

Pronunciation Excercise

[ə] rec**o**gnize, c**o**nditi**o**n,

[ou] r**o**ller, m**o**ld, j**o**ke, g**o**ld, **o**pen

[ʌ] gl**o**ve, l**o**ve, s**o**n, sp**o**nge

[ɔː] glory, fog, thought, bought

[ɑː] pond, pop, jog, job, knock

[ɪ] women

Try it in English

1. 자신의 잠재력을 입증하는 것이 중요하다.

   To ______ your ________ is crucial.

2. 그 선수가 마지막 순간에 골을 넣었다.

   The player ________ the ________ in the last seconds.

3. 학생들은 공상과학영화에 끌리는 것이 보통이다.

   The students are usually attracted to _____- ______ movies.

For Improvement of Your Critical Thinking

Question: Currently, some professional athletes make an incredible amount of money and enjoy tremendous popularity. Are you for the professionalism of sports? Give us your ideas.

Michael Jordan

http://www.youtube.com/watch?v=BOh1cQ61l6w&feature=fvwn

Darren Whitley/The Sporting News

Michael Jeffrey Jordan (born February 17, 1963) is a retired American professional basketball player and active businessman. His biography on the National Basketball Association (NBA) website states, "By acclamation, Michael Jordan is the greatest basketball player of all time." Jordan was one of the most effectively marketed athletes of his generation and was instrumental in popularizing the NBA around the world in the 1980s and 1990s. After a stand-out career at the University of North Carolina at Chapel Hill, where he led the Tar Heels to a National Championship in 1982, Jordan joined the NBA's Chicago Bulls in 1984.

He quickly emerged as a league star, entertaining crowds with his prolific scoring. His leaping ability, illustrated by performing slam dunks from the free throw line at Slam Dunk Contests, earned him the nicknames "Air Jordan" and "His Airness". He also gained a reputation for being one of the best defensive players in basketball. In 1991, he won his first NBA championship with the Bulls, and followed that achievement with titles in 1992 and 1993, securing a "three-peat". Although Jordan abruptly retired from basketball at the beginning of the 1993–94 NBA season to pursue a career in baseball, he rejoined the Bulls in 1995 and led them to three additional championships (1996, 1997, and 1998) as well as an NBA-record 72 regular-season wins in the 1995–96 season. Jordan retired for a second time in 1999, but returned for two more NBA seasons in 2001 as a member of the Washington Wizards.

http://www.wikipedia.org

6 Car Review of New Toyota Prius Hybrid

http://www.youtube.com/watch?v=BpTJi7MK-1s

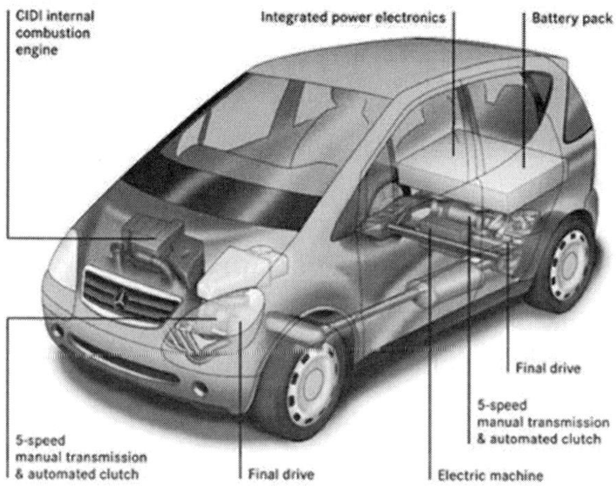

The British Petroleum Oil Refinery in Carson, California. It provides for one quarter of Los Angeles gasoline market, helps give us those famous orange sunsets.

It went on-line in 1938, the same year oil was first discovered in Saudi Arabia, and today it pumps out over 275,000 barrels of black gold each day.

That's enough to get this Toyota Prius from here to the sun and back three times.

So we figured that Prius would be the perfect car to take a little road trip, because frankly we can't afford the gas to do it with anything else.

Along the way, we'll try and figure out if the cult of hybrid really is all it's claimed to be. But one thing is for certain - it sure will be nice to get away from all this.

A journey will take us from the petro-chemical hub of Carson, up Highway 1 to the California state parks of Big Sur. The 11.9 gallon tank is full, and with an estimated 46 mpg, we should have no problem making the 320 mile trip in the Prius with plenty of spare.

Now, the Prius isn't just a hybrid, it's THE hybrid. And it works by just using 1.5 liter 4 cylinder engine. It puts out 76 horses and a pretty measly go 80 pound-feet of torque.

But it's assisted by a permanent magnet AC synchronous electric motor that puts out 67 horses and rather drool-inspiring 295 pound-feet of torque.

Don't get too excited. The Prius optimized for efficiency and not performance, so it won't be winning and stop-light drag races. But it does hold the crown for the newest fuel-efficient car on the American market today.

Key Words & Expressions

cult *noun* an instance of great veneration of a person, ideal, or thing, as manifested by a body of admirers: *the physical fitness cult.*

mpg *acronym* miles per gallon.

measly *adjective* contemptibly small, meager, or slight.

torque *noun* Torque is the tendency of a force to rotate an object about an axis, fulcrum, or pivot. Just as a force is a push or a pull, a torque can be thought of as a twist. In more basic terms, torque measures how hard something is rotated. For example, imagine a wrench or spanner trying to twist a nut or bolt. The amount of "twist" (torque) depends on how long the wrench is, how hard you push down on it, and how well you are pushing it in the correct direction. The terminology for this concept is not straightforward: In physics, it is usually called "torque", and in mechanical engineering, it is called "moment". However, in mechanical engineering, the term "torque" means something different. (http://www.wikipedia.org)

drool *verb* to water at the mouth, as in anticipation of food, salivate.

drag race *noun* a race between two or more automobiles starting from a standstill, the winner being the car that can accelerate the fastest.

Proverbs Related to the Text

- You cannot please everybody.
- Variety is the spice of life.
- Might makes right.

Listen and Fill in the Blanks.

The British Petroleum Oil Refinery in Carson, California. It provides for one quarter of Los Angeles __________ market, helps give us those famous orange sunsets.

It went online in 1938, the same year oil was first discovered in Saudi Arabia, and today it pumps out over 275,000 barrels of _______ ______ each day.

That's enough to get this Toyota Prius from here to the sun and back three times.

So we figured that Prius would be the perfect car to take a little road trip, because frankly we can't afford the gas to do it with anything else.

Along the way, we'll try and figure out if the ______ of hybrid really is all it's claimed to be. But one thing is for certain - it sure will be nice to get away from all this.

A journey will take us from the petro-chemical hub of Carson, up Highway 1 to the California state parks of Big Sur. The 11.9 gallon tank is full, and with an estimated 46 mpg, we should have no problem _________ the 320 mile trip in the Prius with plenty of ________.

Now, the Prius isn't just a hybrid, it's THE hybrid. And it works by just using 1.5 liter 4 cylinder engine. It puts out 76 horses and a pretty _________ go 80 pound-feet of _________.

Pronunciation Bites

한국인 영어발음오류유형 6: 燈下不明

등하불명. 등잔 밑이 어둡다는 말이다. 한국인들이 흔히 범하는 영어 발음 유형에는 영어를 처음 배울 때 접했던 영어 alphabet의 이름이나 영어를 외래어로 쓰는 사례가 빈번해 지면서 일어나는 경우가 있다. 마치 전염병이나 spam mail이 확산되듯이 퍼져 나간 경우이다. 다음의 경우이다.

zed *[zet, ʧet, zetʰɨ, tʃetʰɨ]
basic *[peizik, peiʤik]
staff [stæp, step]

영어 마지막 alphabet인 Z의 글자 이름은 영국인들과 캐나다인들은 [zed], 미국인들의 경우는 [zi:]이다. 영어의 단어 끝 자음에 적용되는 다소의 무성음화를 감안한다 하더라도 한국인들의 발음처럼 완전한 무성음 [t]로 발음하지는 않는다. 유성음으로 발음해야 한다.

Z의 첫소리를 마찰음이 아닌 폐찰음 [ʧ]으로 내는 것은 또 다른 오류로서 한국어에 존재하지 않는 소리 [z]를 대체하여 내는 소리이다. 마찰음으로서 발음연습이 필요하다.

Basic의 경우도 누가 시킨 것도 아닌데 한결같이 [베이지]으로 발음하고 책제목으로도 'ㅇㅇㅇ 베이식' 버젓하게 모습을 드러내고 있다. 분명한 오류로서 [beisik]으로 발음해야 이번에는 철자 <s>의 발음이 유성음이 아닌 무성음 [s]이란 점을 상기해야 한다.

Staff의 경우는 흔히 잘 차려 입은 영화배우들이 무슨 무슨 시상식에서 "[스탭]에게 감사드립니다"라는 말을 자주 하곤 한다. 한국인이면 결코 낯설지 않을 정도로 귀에 익숙한 말이다. 그러나 [스탭]이란 말이 누구를 가리키는 지는 짐작하는 사람이 많겠지만 이 단어의 정확한 어원을 모르고 쓴 경우가 허다하리라 생각된다. 영어의 [stæf]의 마지막 음 마찰음 [f]이 한국어의 음절 종성으로 불가하기 때문에 이를 [p]로 대체한 결과이다.

Pronunciation Excercise

basics. basically, basic questions, basic notions
X, Y and Z (British), from A to Z
administrative staff, faculty and staff, staff members

Try it in English

1. 기름을 가득 채워주세요. (자동차 주유시)

   _________ it ________, please.

2. 과속운전으로 적발되어 딱지를 발급받았다.

   Because of speeding violation, I __________ a ___________.

3. 이 새로 나온 차는 연료효율이 높다.

   This new car model has high _________ ___________.

For Improvement of Your Critical Thinking

Question: Most of us are exceedingly concerned about the energy sources of the future. Everybody seems to accept the gloomy fact that so-called fossil fuels, like petroleum and coal, are running out in the foreseeable future. Here is the question: What will be the most useful substitute energy source to replace fossil fuels? Why?

Hybrid Car

A hybrid electric vehicle (HEV) is a hybrid vehicle that combines a conventional internal combustion engine propulsion system with an electric propulsion system. The presence of the electric power train is intended to achieve better fuel economy than a conventional vehicle. A hybrid electric vehicle is also a form of electric vehicle; a variety of types of HEV exist, and the degree to which they function as EVs varies as well. The most common form of HEV is the hybrid electric car, an automobile driven by a gasoline internal combustion engine (ICE) and electric motors powered by batteries.

Modern HEVs make use of efficiency-improving technologies such as regenerative braking, which converts the vehicle's kinetic energy into battery-replenishing electric energy, rather than wasting it as heat energy as vehicles equipped with conventional brakes do. Some varieties of HEVs use their internal combustion engine to generate electricity by spinning an electrical generator (this combination is known as a motor-generator), to either recharge their batteries or directly feed power to the electric motors that drive the vehicle. Many HEVs reduce idle emissions by shutting down the ICE at idle and restarting it when needed; this is known as a start-stop system. A hybrid-electric produces less emissions from its ICE than a comparably-sized gasoline car, as an HEV's gasoline engine is usually smaller than a pure fossil-fuel vehicle, and if not used to directly drive the car, can be geared to run at maximum efficiency, further improving fuel economy.

http://www.wikipedia.org

7 Fall of the Roman Empire

http://www.youtube.com/watch?v=gJ-GrWpdCE0

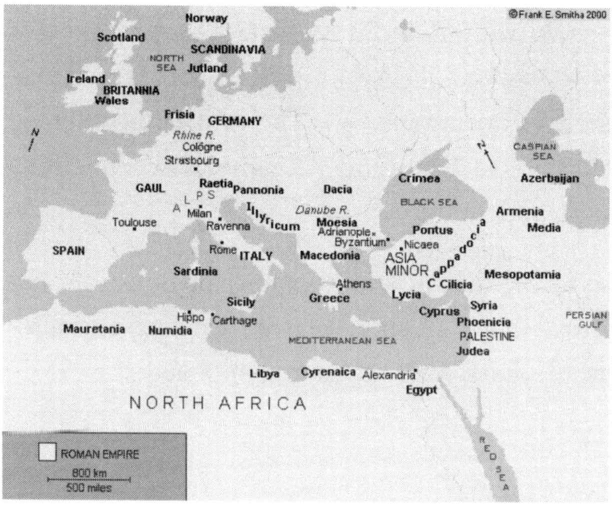

http://www.fsmitha.com/h1/map21rm.htm

Imagine everything civilization: art, culture, wealth, food, education, peace.

Imagine a single nation become a single world. All men living as one citizens of the same land.

Imagine unparalleled heights of human endeavor.

Imagine nothing, nothing. Nothing except fire and pain, anarchy and chaos, destruction and death.

And then, once again, imagine nothing.

Nothing, except isolation, insecurity, fear. utter, utter...

This was what happened when the Roman Empire fell.

Sixteen hundred years ago, civilization stopped, and men stopped and turned back, back to the time of barbarity and pain.

There has never been a greater change in human existence, human condition. Never before have people had so much and had it taken from them so fast. It highlights the fragility of our own being.

But why?

Why did it happen? How could we fall so far so fast? This is what this small documentary will try to explore. There's a lack of debate and discussion within modern historical documentaries. The past is represented as something based upon fact. Most historians actually know something was based upon assumption and opinion

We'll discuss some of these ideas, debate and hopefully demonstrate not just the varied world of history, but also show that it's exciting and alive today as it was thousands of years ago, when it happened.

Key Words & Expressions

unparalleled *adjective* unmatched, not paralleled, unprecedented: *unparalleled poetic ability.*

barbarity *noun* brutal or inhuman conduct.

fragile *adjective* easily broken, shattered, or damaged: *a fragile glass container; a quite fragile alliance.*

be based upon *idiom His plans were based upon a watertight preparation.*

turn back *phrasal verb Let's turn back to page fifty.*

Proverbs Related to the Text

- Rome wasn't built in a day.
- A stitch in time saves nine.
- Misfortunes never come alone.

Listen and Fill in the Blanks.

Imagine everything ________________: art, culture, wealth, __________, education, peace. Imagine a single nation; become a single world. All men living as one ____________ of the ________ ___________. Imagine unparalleled height of human ___________________. Imagine nothing, nothing. Nothing except fire and pain, _______________ and ___________, destruction and death.

And then, once again, imagine nothing.

Pronunciation Bites

한국인 영어발음오류유형 7 : [ɔ:]

한국어의 [오]와 유사한 영어의 발음 [o]는 단모음으로 나타나는 경우는 없고 [ou]의 이중모음 시작모음으로만 나타난다. 예컨대 coat, boat, pole, go, goal은 모두 [ou]의 모음을 가지고 있다. 따라서 영어에서 단독모음으로 [오] 발음은 존재하지 않는다고 보면 된다. 그렇다면 또 다른 한국어의 [오]와 유사한 다음의 경우는 어떤가? 예컨대 cause, lost, cost, pause, law등은 모두 모음이 [ɔ:]이다. 이 모음을 발음하는 요령은 한국어의 [오]와 같이 입술은 오므린 채 아래턱을 낮추어 입이 [어]의 경우보다 벌어지게 취한다. 미국영어의 중서부(midwest), 캐나다 영어 발음의 최근 동향은 [ɔ:]와 [ɑ:]의 발음이 통합된다는 것이다. 이들 중서부 영어는 영어 표준어인 General American의 모태로서 표준어와 진배없기 때문에 한국인들의 경우는 우리가 발음하기 쉬운 [ɑ:]로 통일하여 발음하는 것도 영어발음법의 한 요령이라고 볼 수 있다. 다음의 경우를 연습해 보자.

Pronunciation Excercise

a. boat, coat, most, postcard, low, bowl, low

b. boss, pot, cot, lobby

c. lost, loss, cost, because, law

다시 한 번 말하면 (b)와 (c)의 모음을 동일하게 [ɑ:]로 발음하는 경향이 미국의 동부, 남부지역을 제외한 나머지 지역과 캐나다 지역의 발음으로 정착되어 가고 있다. 한국인들은 양쪽 발음을 한국어의 [아]를 좀 길게 발음한 상태로 조음하면 문제가 없다. [오] 보다는 [아]가 영어발음에 가깝다는 점을 명심할 필요가 있다.

여기서 영국영어 특히 전통적으로 영국의 표준발음으로 인정해온 'Received Pronunciation'(RP)의 경우를 언급하지 않을 수 없다. 한국에도 미국 일변도의 영어발음학습에 문제가 있다고 보고 다양한 세계 영어의 말투에 관심을 보이기 시작하고 있다. 여기서는 위에서 든 예 중에서 (b)의 경우가 영국영어에서 미국의 영어와 뚜렷한 차이를 보인다고 하지만 한국어 화자에게는 정확한 음가를 파악하기 쉽지 않다. 일단 국제음성기호로는 [ɒ]로 나타내는 특이한 소리이다. 국제음성기호 (IPA) 모음도표의 맨 아래 오른쪽 귀퉁이에 위치한 모음이다. 다시 말해서 조음위치는 혀의 몸체를 최대한 후퇴시키고 동시에 낮추되 입술은 오므린 상태를 유지해야 이 소리가 난다. 따라서 한국어의 [오] 보다 혀의 위치가 훨씬 낮은 소리이며 [ɑ:]와 다른 점은 [ɑ:]와는 달리 입술을 오므린다는 점과 길이가 짧다는 점이다. 영국영어를 오랜 기간 동안 사용해온 화자가 아니면 조음하기 매우 까다로우며 한국인들은 잘못하여 영국인들의 이 발음을 한국어의 [오]에 대응시키는 오류를 범하기 쉬운 모음이다.

Try it in English

1. 네 생각은 오해에서 비롯된 것이다.
   Your idea was _________ ________ misunderstanding.

2. 과거로 되돌아가지 말라.
   Don't __________ ____________ to the past.

For Improvement of Your Critical Thinking

Question: The Roman Empire prospered and achieved unprecedented civilization. However, it underwent an unavoidable decay and helplessly collapsed. Do you think every nation or culture which has once enjoyed outstanding accomplishments is doomed to failure in the long run? If yes, why?

Views on Rise and Fall of Roman Empire

Edward Gibbon : *The History of the Decline and Fall of the Roman Empire*

Gibbon offers an explanation for why the Roman Empire fell, a task made difficult by a lack of comprehensive written sources, though he was not the only historian to tackle the subject. Most of his ideas are directly taken from what few relevant records were available: those of the Roman moralists of the 4th and 5th centuries. According to Gibbon, the Roman Empire succumbed to barbarian invasions in large part due to the gradual loss of civic virtue among its citizens. They had become weak, outsourcing their duties to defend their Empire to barbarian mercenaries, who then became so numerous and ingrained that they were able to take over the Empire. Romans, he believed, had become effeminate, unwilling to live a tougher, "manly" military lifestyle. He further blames the degeneracy of the Roman army and the Praetorian guards. In addition, Gibbon argued that Christianity created a belief that a better life existed after death, which fostered an indifference to the present among Roman citizens, thus sapping their desire to sacrifice for the Empire. He also believed its comparative pacifism tended to hamper the traditional Roman martial spirit. Lastly, like other Enlightenment thinkers, Gibbon held in contempt the Middle Ages as a priest-ridden, superstitious, dark age. It was not until his own age of reason and rational thought, it was believed, that human history could resume its progress.

Arnold Toynbee : *A Study of History*

Arnold Joseph Toynbee (1889~1975) was a British historian whose twelve-volume analysis of the rise and fall of civilizations, A Study of History, 1934-1961, was a synthesis of world history, a metahistory based on universal rhythms of rise, flowering and decline, which examined history from a global perspective.Toynbee's ideas and approach to history may be said to fall into the discipline of Comparative history. While they may be compared to those used by Oswald Spengler in The Decline of the West, he rejected Spengler's deterministic view that civilizations rise and fall according to a natural and inevitable cycle.. He identified his civilizations according to cultural or religious rather than national criteria. With the civilizations as units identified, he presented the history of each in terms of challenge-and-response. Civilizations arose in response to some set of challenges of extreme difficulty, when "creative minorities" devised solutions that reoriented their entire society. Challenges and responses were physical, as when the Sumerians exploited the intractable swamps of southern Iraq by organizing the Neolithic inhabitants into a society capable of carrying out large-scale irrigation projects; or social, as when the Catholic Church resolved the chaos of post-Roman Europe by enrolling the new Germanic kingdoms in a single religious community. (http://www.wikipedia.org)

8 Harvard Commencement Speech 2008 by J. K. Rowling

The Fringe Benefits of Failure, and the Importance of Imagination

http://harvardmagazine.com/commencement/the-fringe-benefits-failure-the-importance-imagination

J.K. Rowling, author of the best-selling *Harry Potter* book series, delivers her Commencement Address, "The Fringe Benefits of Failure, and the Importance of Imagination," at the Annual Meeting of the Harvard Alumni Association.(http://www.harvard.edu)

President Faust, members of the Harvard Corporation and the Board of Overseers, members of the faculty, proud parents, and, above all, graduates.

The first thing I would like to say is 'thank you.' Not only has Harvard given me an extraordinary honour, but the weeks of fear and nausea I have endured at the thought of giving this commencement address have made me lose weight. A win-win situation! Now all I have to do is take deep breaths, squint at the red banners and convince myself that I am at the world's largest Gryffindor reunion.

Delivering a commencement address is a great responsibility; or so I thought until I cast my mind back to my own graduation. The commencement speaker that day was the distinguished British philosopher Baroness Mary Warnock. Reflecting on her speech has helped me enormously in writing this one, because it turns out that I can't remember a single word she said. This liberating discovery enables me to proceed without any fear that I might inadvertently influence you to abandon promising careers in business, the law or politics for the giddy delights of becoming a gay wizard.

You see? If all you remember in years to come is the 'gay wizard' joke, I've come out ahead of Baroness Mary Warnock. Achievable goals: the first step to self improvement.

Actually, I have wracked my mind and heart for what I ought to say to you today. I have asked myself what I wish I had known at my own graduation, and what important lessons I have learned in the 21 years that have expired between that day and this.

I have come up with two answers. On this wonderful day when we are gathered together to celebrate your academic success, I have decided to talk to you about the benefits of failure. And as you stand on the threshold of what is sometimes called 'real life', I want to extol the crucial importance of imagination.

These may seem quixotic or paradoxical choices, but please bear with me.

Looking back at the 21-year-old that I was at graduation, is a slightly uncomfortable experience for the 42-year-old that she has become. Half my lifetime ago, I was striking an uneasy balance between the ambition I had for myself, and what those closest to me expected of me.

I was convinced that the only thing I wanted to do, ever, was to write novels. However, my parents, both of whom came from impoverished backgrounds and neither of whom had been to college, took the view that my overactive imagination was an amusing personal quirk that would never pay a mortgage, or secure a pension. I know that the irony strikes with the force of a cartoon anvil, now.

So they hoped that I would take a vocational degree; I wanted to study English Literature. A compromise was reached that in retrospect satisfied nobody, and I went up to study Modern Languages. Hardly had my parents' car rounded the corner at the end of the road than I ditched German and scuttled off down the Classics corridor.

I cannot remember telling my parents that I was studying Classics; they might well have found out for the first time on graduation day. Of all the subjects on this planet, I think they would have been hard put to name one less useful than Greek mythology when it came to securing the keys to an executive bathroom.

I would like to make it clear, in parenthesis, that I do not blame my parents for their point of view. There is an expiry date on blaming your parents for steering you in the wrong direction; the moment you are old enough to take the wheel, responsibility lies with you. What is more, I cannot criticise my parents for hoping that I would never experience poverty. They had been poor themselves, and I have since been poor, and I quite agree with them that it is not an ennobling experience. Poverty entails fear, and stress, and sometimes depression; it means a thousand petty humiliations and hardships. Climbing out of poverty by your own efforts, that is indeed something on which to pride yourself, but poverty itself is romanticised only by fools.

What I feared most for myself at your age was not poverty, but failure.

At your age, in spite of a distinct lack of motivation at university, where I had spent far too long in the coffee bar writing stories, and far too little time at lectures, I had a knack for passing examinations, and that, for years, had been the measure of success in my life and that of my peers.

I am not dull enough to suppose that because you are young, gifted and well-educated, you have never known hardship or heartbreak. Talent and intelligence never yet inoculated anyone against the caprice of the

Fates, and I do not for a moment suppose that everyone here has enjoyed an existence of unruffled privilege and contentment.

However, the fact that you are graduating from Harvard suggests that you are not very well-acquainted with failure. You might be driven by a fear of failure quite as much as a desire for success. Indeed, your conception of failure might not be too far from the average person's idea of success, so high have you already flown.

Ultimately, we all have to decide for ourselves what constitutes failure, but the world is quite eager to give you a set of criteria if you let it. So I think it fair to say that by any conventional measure, a mere seven years after my graduation day, I had failed on an epic scale. An exceptionally short-lived marriage had imploded, and I was jobless, a lone parent, and as poor as it is possible to be in modern Britain, without being homeless. The fears that my parents had had for me, and that I had had for myself, had both come to pass, and by every usual standard, I was the biggest failure I knew.

Now, I am not going to stand here and tell you that failure is fun. That period of my life was a dark one, and I had no idea that there was going to be what the press has since represented as a kind of fairy tale resolution. I had no idea then how far the tunnel extended, and for a long time, any light at the end of it was a hope rather than a reality.

So why do I talk about the benefits of failure? Simply because failure meant a stripping away of the inessential. I stopped pretending to myself that I was anything other than what I was, and began to direct all my energy into finishing the only work that mattered to me. Had I really succeeded at anything else, I might never have found the determination to succeed in the one arena I believed I truly belonged. I was set free, because my greatest fear had been realised, and I was still alive, and I still had a daughter whom I adored, and I had an old typewriter and a big idea. And so rock bottom became the solid foundation on which I rebuilt my life.

You might never fail on the scale I did, but some failure in life is inevitable. It is impossible to live without failing at something, unless you live so cautiously that you might as well not have lived at all – in which case, you fail by default.

Failure gave me an inner security that I had never attained by passing examinations. Failure taught me things about myself that I could have learned no other way. I discovered that I had a strong will, and more discipline than I had suspected; I also found out that I had friends whose value was truly above the price of rubies.

The knowledge that you have emerged wiser and stronger from setbacks means that you are, ever after, secure in your ability to survive. You will never truly know yourself, or the strength of your relationships, until both have been tested by adversity. Such knowledge is a true gift, for all that it is painfully won, and it has been worth more than any qualification I ever earned.

So given a Time Turner, I would tell my 21-year-old self that personal happiness lies in knowing that life is not a check-list of acquisition or achievement. Your qualifications, your CV, are not your life, though you will meet many people of my age and older who confuse the two. Life is difficult, and complicated, and beyond anyone's total control, and the humility to know that will enable you to survive its vicissitudes.

Now you might think that I chose my second theme, the importance of imagination, because of the part it played in rebuilding my life, but that is not wholly so. Though I personally will defend the value of bedtime stories to my last gasp, I have learned to value imagination in a much broader sense. Imagination is not only the uniquely human capacity to envision that which is not, and therefore the fount of all invention and innovation. In its arguably most transformative and revelatory capacity, it is the power that enables us to empathise with humans whose experiences we have never shared.

One of the greatest formative experiences of my life preceded Harry Potter, though it informed much of what I subsequently wrote in those books. This revelation came in the form of one of my earliest day jobs.

Though I was sloping off to write stories during my lunch hours, I paid the rent in my early 20s by working at the African research department at Amnesty International's headquarters in London.

There in my little office I read hastily scribbled letters smuggled out of totalitarian regimes by men and women who were risking imprisonment to inform the outside world of what was happening to them. I saw photographs of those who had disappeared without trace, sent to Amnesty by their desperate families and friends. I read the testimony of torture victims and saw pictures of their injuries. I opened handwritten, eye-witness accounts of summary trials and executions, of kidnappings and rapes.

Many of my co-workers were ex-political prisoners, people who had been displaced from their homes, or fled into exile, because they had the temerity to speak against their governments. Visitors to our offices included those who had come to give information, or to try and find out what had happened to those they had left behind.

I shall never forget the African torture victim, a young man no older than I was at the time, who had become mentally ill after all he had endured in his homeland. He trembled uncontrollably as he spoke into a video camera about the brutality inflicted upon him. He was a foot taller than I was, and seemed as fragile as a child. I was given the job of escorting him back to the Underground Station afterwards, and this man whose life had been shattered by cruelty took my hand with exquisite courtesy, and wished me future happiness.

And as long as I live I shall remember walking along an empty corridor and suddenly hearing, from behind a closed door, a scream of pain and horror such as I have never heard since. The door opened, and the researcher poked out her head and told me to run and make a hot drink for the young man sitting with her. She had just had to give him the news that in retaliation for his own outspokenness against his country's regime, his mother had been seized and executed.

Every day of my working week in my early 20s I was reminded how incredibly fortunate I was, to live in a country with a democratically elected government, where legal representation and a public trial were the rights of everyone.

Every day, I saw more evidence about the evils humankind will inflict on their fellow humans, to gain or maintain power. I began to have nightmares, literal nightmares, about some of the things I saw, heard, and read.

And yet I also learned more about human goodness at Amnesty International than I had ever known before.

Amnesty mobilises thousands of people who have never been tortured or imprisoned for their beliefs to act on behalf of those who have. The power of human empathy, leading to collective action, saves lives, and frees prisoners. Ordinary people, whose personal well-being and security are assured, join together in huge numbers to save people they do not know, and will never meet. My small participation in that process was one of the most humbling and inspiring experiences of my life.

Unlike any other creature on this planet, humans can learn and understand, without having experienced. They can think themselves into other people's places.

Of course, this is a power, like my brand of fictional magic, that is morally neutral. One might use such an ability to manipulate, or control, just as much as to understand or sympathise.

And many prefer not to exercise their imaginations at all. They choose to remain comfortably within the bounds of their own experience, never troubling to wonder how it would feel to have been born other than they are. They can refuse to hear screams or to peer inside cages; they can close their minds and hearts to any suffering that does not touch them personally; they can refuse to know.

I might be tempted to envy people who can live that way, except that I do not think they have any fewer nightmares than I do. Choosing to live in narrow spaces leads to a form of mental agoraphobia, and that brings its own terrors. I think the wilfully unimaginative see more monsters. They are often more afraid.

What is more, those who choose not to empathise enable real monsters. For without ever committing an act of outright evil ourselves, we collude with it, through our own apathy.

One of the many things I learned at the end of that Classics corridor down which I ventured at the age of 18, in search of something I could not then define, was this, written by the Greek author Plutarch: What we achieve inwardly will change outer reality.

That is an astonishing statement and yet proven a thousand times every day of our lives. It expresses, in part, our inescapable connection with the outside world, the fact that we touch other people's lives simply by existing.

But how much more are you, Harvard graduates of 2008, likely to touch other people's lives? Your intelligence, your capacity for hard work, the education you have earned and received, give you unique status, and unique responsibilities. Even your nationality sets you apart. The great majority of you belong to the world's only remaining superpower. The way you vote, the way you live, the way you protest, the pressure you bring to bear on your government, has an impact way beyond your borders. That is your privilege, and your burden.

If you choose to use your status and influence to raise your voice on behalf of those who have no voice; if you choose to identify not only with the powerful, but with the powerless; if you retain the ability to imagine yourself into the lives of those who do not have your advantages, then it will not only be your proud families who celebrate your existence, but thousands and millions of people whose reality you have helped change. We do not need magic to change the world, we carry all the power we need inside ourselves already: we have the power to imagine better.

I am nearly finished. I have one last hope for you, which is something that I already had at 21. The friends with whom I sat on graduation day have been my friends for life. They are my children's godparents, the people to whom I've been able to turn in times of trouble, people who have been kind enough not to sue me when I took their names for Death Eaters. At our graduation we were bound by enormous affection, by our shared experience of a time that could never come again, and, of course, by the knowledge that we held certain photographic evidence that would be exceptionally valuable if any of us ran for Prime Minister.

So today, I wish you nothing better than similar friendships. And tomorrow, I hope that even if you remember not a single word of mine, you remember those of Seneca, another of those old Romans I met when I fled down the Classics corridor, in retreat from career ladders, in search of ancient wisdom:
As is a tale, so is life: not how long it is, but how good it is, is what matters.
I wish you all very good lives.
Thank you very much.

Key Words & Expressions

fringe benefit *noun* Fringe benefits are compensations made to an employee beyond the regular benefit of being paid for their work, such as offering a few days of sick time or paid vacation time.

nausea *noun* sickness at the stomach when followed by a loathing for food and an involuntary impulse to vomit.

squint *verb* to look with the eyes partly closed.

Gryffindor *noun* Gryffindor values courage, bravery, daring, nerve and chivalry. Its mascot is the lion, and its colours are red and gold. The Head of this house is the Transfiguration teacher, Minerva McGonagall, and the house ghost is Nearly Headless Nick. According to Rowling, Gryffindor corresponds roughly to the element of fire. The founder of the house is Godric Gryffindor. Though Gryffindor is the house of most of the major protagonists, not all Gryffindors fall into that category. Cormac McLaggen is the negative qualities of Gryffindor personified; he is ill-tempered and pushy. Romilda Vane is underhanded and displays a deceptive and devious nature by trying unsuccessfully to ply Harry with a love potion. On the Hogwarts Express, she is somewhat condescending towards Neville Longbottom and Luna Lovegood. However, both McLaggen and Vane certainly are bold, and show confidence, two very Gryffindor qualities, and were therefore sorted into the house. Peter Pettigrew, a Death Eater, also went into this house.The Gryffindor common room is located in one of the castle's highest towers, the entrance to which is located on the seventh floor in the east wing of the castle and is guarded by a painting of The Fat Lady, who is garbed in a pink dress. (http:www.wikipedia.org)

Mary Warnock (born 14 April 1924) a British philosopher of morality, education and mind, and writer on existentialism.

giddy *adjective* attended with or causing dizziness: *a giddy cliff.*

wrack *verb* damage or destruction: *wrack and ruin.*

extol *verb* to praise highly, eulogize: *to extol the beauty of Rio de Janeiro.*

quixotic *adjective* resembling or befitting Don Quixote.

quirk *noun* a peculiarity of action, behavior, or personality: *They are full of intense quirks.*

cartoon anvil *noun* Anvil cartoons from the CartoonStock directory — the world's largest on-line collection of cartoons.

ditch *verb* to escape from: *He ditched the cops by driving down an alley.*

scuttle off *phrasal verb* to run with quick, hasty steps, scurry.

expiry date *noun* an alternative term for expiration date.

knack *noun* a special skill, talent, or aptitude: He had a knack for saying the funny thing.

inoculate *verb* to implant a disease agent or antigen in a person, animal, for study or to stimulate disease resistance.

caprice *noun* an unpredictable change, as of one's mind or the weather.

unruffled *adjective* calm, not emotionally upset or agitated, steady: *He became pretty excited, but she stayed unruffled.*

epic *adjective* of great size or extent: a crime rate of epic proportions.

setback *noun* a check to progress: *The new rule met a setback.*

empathize *verb* to experience empathy: *Her skill to empathize with people made him an excellent marriage counselor.*

slope off *phrasal verb* to make one's way out slowly or furtively.

Amnesty International *noun* an international non-governmental organisation which defines its mission as "to conduct research and generate action to prevent and end grave abuses of human rights and to demand justice for those whose rights have been violated." Founded in London, England in 1961, AI draws its attention to human rights abuses and campaigns for compliance with international standards. It works to mobilise public opinion which exerts pressure on individuals who perpetrate abuses. The organization was awarded the 1977 Nobel Peace Prize for its "campaign against torture and the United Nations Prize in the Field of Human Rights in 1978. (http://www.wikipedia.org)

temerity *noun* reckless boldness, rashness.

peer *verb* to look narrowly or searchingly.

agoraphobia *noun* an abnormal fear of being in crowds, public places, or open areas.

collude *verb* to act together through a secret understanding with evil intent.

Proverbs Related to the Text

- Imagination is the fount of all invention and innovation.
- What we achieve inwardly will change outer reality.
- As is a tale, so is life: not how long it is, but how good it is, is what matters.

Listen and Fill in the Blanks.

One of the greatest ____________ experiences of my life preceded Harry Potter, though it informed much of what I subsequently wrote in those books. This revelation ___________ in the form of one of my earliest day jobs. Though I was sloping off to write stories during my lunch hours, I paid the rent ____ ____ _______ ________ by working at the African research department at Amnesty International's headquarters in London.

There in my little office I read hastily scribbled letters __________ out of totalitarian regimes by men and women who were __________ imprisonment to inform the outside world of what was happening to them. I saw photographs of those who had disappeared ________ ________, sent to Amnesty by their desperate families and friends. I read the testimony of torture victims and saw pictures of their injuries. I opened handwritten, eye-witness accounts of summary trials and executions, of kidnappings and rapes.

Many of my ____________ were ____________ prisoners, people who had been displaced from their homes, or fled into exile, because they had the temerity to speak against their governments. Visitors to our offices included those who had come to give information, or to try and find out what had happened to those they had ________ ________.

Pronunciation Bites

한국인 영어발음오류유형 8 : 단어강세

단어강세는 영어와 한국어의 관계가 다른 발음오류의 경우와는 성격을 달리한다. 다른 유형의 오류들의 기원은 모국어인 한국어의 소리체계나 소리현상의 영향으로 인한 것이라고 볼 수 있다. 그러나 단어강세의 경우는 한국어에서 역할에 관하여 논란이 있기는 하지만 역할이 뚜렷하지 않다. 만일 한국어에 단어강세가 전혀 존재하지 않는다고 가정한다면 영어강세의 오류가 한국어에서 기원한다는 가설은 성립되지 않는다. 아무튼 한국인의 영어 단어강세 유형은 다음과 같이 나타나고 있다.

첫째, 2음절 이상의 단어에서 우리는 무의식중에 영어 단어를 모조리 첫 음절에 강세를 주려는 경향이 있다. 요행히 맞는 경우도 많지만 다음의 경우는 앞에서 두 번째 음절에 강세가 오는 점을 주의해야 한다. 여타 오류유형에서 언급한 바와 같이 강세의 오류는 리듬의 오류, 모음, 자음의 오류를 필연적으로 동반하게 되므로 사태의 심각성이 있다는 점을 명심할 필요가 있다.

Pronunciation Excercise 1

eclipse
McDonald's
celebrity
Korea/career
guerilla/gorilla
America

두 번째, 영어 단어강세는 파생어와 어근/어간의 강세와 동일한 경우와 그렇지 않은 경우를 구분해야 한다. 양쪽을 구분하지 않고 어근/어간과 파생어를 동일하게 발음하는 경향이 있다. 예컨대 origin/original/originality의 파생과정에서 강세는 어근 origin에서 접미사 –al이 붙으면 둘째 음절에 강세가 오며 다시 접미사 –ity가 붙으면 앞에서 4번째 음절로 강세가 후퇴한다. 다음의 경우 접미사 –al, -ic, -ian, -ity, -ation, 등은 어근/어간의 강세를 뒤쪽으로 후퇴시키는 역할을 한다.

Pronunciation Excercise 2

habit/habitual
atom/atomic, Italy/Italic
Canada/Canadian
divine/divinity, profane/profanity
allege/allegation

반대로 접미사 –ly, -ness, -less, -al(명사), -ship, -y(형용사)는 어근/어간의 강세의 변화를 가져오지 않는다. 이 경우는 오류가 거의 발견되지 않는다.

Pronunciation Excercise 3

shrewd/shrewdly, prudent/prudently
unusual/unusualness
speech/speechless
arrive/arrival
member/membership
feather/feathery

Try it in English

1. 추가급여는 생활에 큰 도움이 된다.

   ________ _________ are much helpful to our daily lives.

2. 금년 농사는 큰 흉작이다.

   This year's __________ are a failure ______ an ______ _______.

3. 이상과 현실의 균형을 맞추기 쉽지 않다.

   It's not easy ______ a _________ between the ideal and the real.

For Improvement of Your Critical Thinking

Question: J. K. Rowling stressed in the speech that she was enormously influenced by Greek mythology and experiences at the office of Amnesty International. What have been the most influential events or experiences that have affected you?

J.K. Rowling

Joanne "Jo" Murray OBE (née Rowling; born 31 July 1965), who writes under the pen name J. K. Rowling, is a British author best known as the creator of the Harry Potter fantasy series, the idea for which was conceived whilst on a train trip from Manchester to London in 1990. The Potter books have gained worldwide attention, won multiple awards, and sold more than 400 million copies.

Aside from writing the Potter novels, Rowling is perhaps equally famous for her "rags to riches" life story, in which she progressed from living on welfare to multi-millionaire status within five years. The 2008 Sunday Times Rich List estimated Rowling's fortune at £560 million ($798 million), ranking her as the twelfth richest woman in Britain. *Forbes* ranked Rowling as the forty-eighth most powerful celebrity of 2007, and Time magazine named her as a runner-up for its 2007 Person of the Year, noting the social, moral, and political inspiration she has given her fandom. She has become a notable philanthropist, supporting such charities as Comic Relief, One Parent Families, Multiple Sclerosis Society of Great Britain, and the Children's High Level Group.

Harry Potter Series

"Harry Potter" is a series of seven fantasy novels written by British author J. K. Rowling. The books chronicle the adventures of the adolescent wizard Harry Potter, together with Ron Weasley and Hermione Granger, his friends from the Hogwarts School of Witchcraft and Wizardry. The central story arc concerns Harry's struggle against the evil wizard Lord Voldemort, who killed Harry's parents in his quest to conquer the wizarding world and subjugate non-magical (Muggle) people to his rule. Several successful derivative films, video games and other themed merchandise have been based upon the series.

Since the 1997 release of the first novel *Harry Potter and the Philosopher's Stone*, which was retitled *Harry Potter and the Sorcerer's Stone* in the United States, the books have gained immense popularity, critical acclaim and commercial success worldwide. As of June 2008, the book series has sold more than 400 million copies and has been translated into 67 languages, and the last four books have consecutively set records as the fastest-selling books in history.

English-language versions of the books are published by Bloomsbury in the United Kingdom, Scholastic Press in the United States, Allen & Unwin in Australia, and Raincoast Books in Canada. Thus far, the first six books have been made into a series of motion pictures by Warner Bros., with the sixth, *Harry Potter and the Half-Blood Prince*, released on 15 July 2009. The series also originated much tie-in merchandise, making the Harry Potter brand worth £15 billion.

1. *Harry Potter and the Philosopher's Stone* (26 June 1997)
2. *Harry Potter and the Chamber of Secrets* (2 July 1998)
3. *Harry Potter and the Prisoner of Azkaban* (8 July 1999)
4. *Harry Potter and the Goblet of Fire* (8 July 2000)
5. *Harry Potter and the Order of the Phoenix* (21 June 2003)
6. *Harry Potter and the Half-Blood Prince* (16 July 2005)
7. *Harry Potter and the Deathly Hallows* (21 July 2007)

www.wikipedia.org

9 The Wright Brothers

http://www.youtube.com/watch?v=qo0kpCU03-U&feature=fvsr

The first flight in 1903 by the Wright Brothers, Kitty Hawk, North Carolina
(http://gardenofpraise.com/ibdwrigh.htm)

A century ago on the sands of Kitty Hawk, two brothers, Wilbur and Olville Wright, bicycle mechanics and inventors built flying machines which would transform our world.

Today, as we mark the centennial of the Wrights' great achievement, a team of modern pilots and aircraft builders have become aviation detectives, tracking the Wright brothers' twelve years of experiment, innovation and genuine risk, which would create the modern airplane.

It feels great! It's flying nice and level. It feels really good!

Starting with simple kites on a beach, in only a dozen years, the Wright brothers built an aircraft which managed to cross the continent.

You'll study the photographs and study the photographs. And at some point, you make a breakthrough. And that breakthrough is…Ah!... This is how they were thinking about this. This is what they thought. Those are wonderful moments.

With modern computer technology and one-hundred-year-old artifacts, the Wright's secrets are pried from history. Lost skills will need to be relearned in order to solve the mysteries of early aviation.

The engine is authentic in every way. It's the only functioning Wright artifact that survives. It's actually, I would say, a national treasure.

Here, it's coming off. And ground's coming off.

More than just inventors, the Wright brothers were also among the world's first test pilots. If today's builders are going to underse and the Wrights' aircrafts, they'll have to take a risk and fly them.

Two men came to try something that half the world believed wasn't even possible. They took great risks, and they were entering an area of the unknown.

Don't hug me like I'm gonna die. You're scaring me!

Accidents were the norm because they were pushing the envelope. All the exhibition teams but one or two were killed in given demonstrations with Wright airplanes.

History shows that piloting Wrights' flyers should be hazardous to your health. Modern flight simulator can limit but not eliminate, the risks.

I've dreamt a lot about being in this airplane and actually flying it, so hopefully, we can make that dream come true.

But as the dreams of the early fliers take shape, questions remain unanswered. And in any airplane, a dream can quickly become a nightmare.

We could hear the airplane running, and then we couldn't hear it.

(An emergency siren and helicopter noise) Nine-one-one, what is your emergency?

We heard it crack and a dart fire and then could hear it going down.

Fasten your seatbelts as NOVA takes a wild ride through aviation's first turbulent decade, unlocking the secrets of the Wright brothers.

On the tarmac at Washington's Dulles Airport, a modern airline pilot performs one of aviation's oldest ritual: a walk-around inspection of his aircraft. Checking for loose fittings, simple nicks and dents, a pilot is ultimately responsible for every aspect of his flight.

Ken Hyde is more than a pilot. He is also a historian of aviation. Long before airplanes had radios and computers, the pilot was the master of his craft, an idea born in the mind of Wilbur and Olville Wright.

How the Wright brothers managed to design, construct, and pilot their aircraft has remained a marvel for over a century. It's Ken Hyde's dream to build and fly the earliest airplane to recreate the genius of the Wright brothers.

Key Words & Expressions

911 the emergency medical number in the United States.

NOVA *noun* a name of a scientific television show.

centennial *adjective* pertaining to a 100th anniversary.

breakthrough *noun* any significant or sudden advance, development, as in scientific knowledge or diplomacy: *The Boeing jet engine was a major breakthrough in air transportation.*

pry *verb* look closely or curiously, peep.

hazardous *adjective* full of risk, risky: *a hazardous journey.*

dart fire *noun* fire with a swift movement like a dart.

nicks and dents grooves and hollows.

walk around inspection an airplane inspection by pilots, looking at the tires and pressures, as well as the general condition of the airplane, trying to catch anything out of place, such as open panels, fuel or hydraulic leaks, or dents and scratches. (http:www.wikipedia.com)

push the envelope *idiom* to stretch established limits, as in technological advance or social innovation.

Proverbs Related to the Text

- Great oaks from little acorns grow.
- He that will eat the kernel must crack the nut.
- The higher the mountain, the greater descent.

Listen and Fill in the Blanks.

A century ago on the ___________ of Kitty Hawk, two brothers, Wilbur and Olville Wright, bicycle mechanics and inventors built flying machines which would transform our world.

Today, as we ___________ centennial of the Wrights' great achievement, a team of modern pilots and aircraft builders have become aviation _______________,

tracking the Wright brothers' twelve years of experiment, innovation and _________ risk, which ________ create the modern airplane.
It feels great! It's nice and level. It feels really good!
Starting with simple kites on a beach, in only a dozen years, the Wright brothers built an aircraft which __________ ______ cross the continent.

Pronunciation Bites
한국인 영어발음오류유형 9 : 격음과 경음

영어 폐쇄음 /p, t, k/는 단어의 위치에 따라 음가가 달라진다. (a)와 같이 강세음절 두음이나 단어의 첫 소리일 경우는 한국어의 격음 /ㅍ,ㅌ,ㅋ/과 유사하고 다른 위치에서는 (b)와 같이 한국어의 경음 /ㅃ, ㄸ, ㄲ/과 유사한 음가로 실현된다. 다음을 연습해 보자.

Pronunciation Excercise

a. pass, Tess, kiss, appear, atone, accord
b. span, style, ski, open, apple, Saturn, Jupiter, acorn, people, open

한국인의 영어발음을 관찰해 보면 위치에 관계없이 항상 한국어의 격음에 가까운 /ㅍ, ㅌ, ㅋ/으로 발음하는 것을 볼 수 있다. 영어 발음에서 강세의 위치가 이 경우에도 중요한 변수로 작용하고 있다는 점을 주의해야 한다. 사실 격음과 경음의 구분은 이러한 구분이 없는 언어 예컨대 불어, 러시아어, 스페인어, 이태리어, 화란어, 일본어 화자에게는 매우 지각하기 힘든 차이이기 때문에 좀처럼 제대로 발음하기 어렵다. 그러나 한국인은 다르다. 한국어 사용자 치고 격음과 경음을 구분하지 못하는 사람은 없다. 그럼에도 영어를 할 때는 충분히 구분이 가능함에도 불구하고 이를 무시하는 경향이 있다. 이유는 연구 대상이고 논란이 있지만 아무튼 한국인에게 가능한 구분이어서 조금만 관심을 기울이면 극복할 수 있는 문제임에 틀림없다.

Try it in English

1. 어제 그럭저럭 숙제를 마쳤다.

   I __________ ________ finish my homework.

2. 이 차의 쭈그러진 곳을 고치는데 3만원 듭니다.

   It __________ 30,000 won to fix the ________ and ________ of this car.

For Improvement of Your Critical Thinking

Question: It is well known that the Wright brothers grasped the mechanical skills essential for flight from working in their bicycle shop. Aside from the Wright brothers many of great inventors in human history developed their skills from their own work rather than from sophisticated experiments in the decent lab. Why do you think some major creations by humans were not done in a classroom or academic environment?

Wright Brothers and the First Airplane

The Wright brothers, Orville (August 19, 1871~January 30, 1948) and Wilbur (April 16, 1867~May 30, 1912), were two Americans who are generally credited with inventing and building the world's first successful airplane and making the first controlled, powered and sustained heavier-than-air human flight, on December 17, 1903. They are also officially credited worldwide through the Fédération Aéronautique Internationale, the standard-setting and record-keeping body for aeronautics and astronautics, as "the first sustained and controlled heavier-than-air powered flight." In the two years afterward, the brothers developed their flying machine into the first practical fixed-wing aircraft. Although not the first to build and fly experimental aircraft, the Wright brothers were the first to invent aircraft controls that made fixed wing flight possible.

The brothers' fundamental breakthrough was their invention of three-axis control, which enabled the pilot to steer the aircraft effectively and to maintain its equilibrium. This method became standard and remains standard on fixed wing aircraft of all kinds. From the beginning of their aeronautical work, the Wright brothers focused on unlocking the secrets of control to conquer "the flying problem," rather than developing more powerful engines as some other experimenters did. Their careful wind tunnel tests produced better aeronautical data than any before, enabling them to design and build wings and propellers more effective than any before. Their U.S. patent 821,393 claims the invention of a system of aerodynamic control that manipulates a flying machine's surfaces.

They gained the mechanical skills essential for their success by working for years in their shop with printing presses, bicycles, motors, and other machinery. Their work with bicycles in particular influenced their belief that an unstable vehicle like a flying machine could be controlled and balanced with practice. From 1900 until their first powered flights in late 1903, they conducted extensive glider tests that also developed their skills as pilots. Their bicycle shop employee Charlie Taylor became an important part of the team, building their first aircraft engine in close collaboration with the brothers.

The Wright brothers' status as inventors of the airplane has been subject to counter-claims by various parties. (http://www.wikipedia.org)

10 Snoopy

http://www.youtube.com/watch?v=pq9hBEvFNIM

No, No, No.

Listen, all of you!

You've got to take direction.

You've got to have discipline.

You've got to have respect for your director.

I oughta slug you.

Ugh! I've been kissed by a dog.

I have dog germs!

Get hot water!

Get some disinfectant.

Get some iodine!

Ah!

Key Words & Expressions

oughta *auxiliary* an informal form of *ought to.*

iodine *noun* a nonmetallic halogen element occurring at ordinary temperatures as a grayish-black crystalline solid.

slug *verb* to strike heavily, hit hard, especially with the fist.

disinfectant *noun* any chemical agent used chiefly on inanimate objects to destroy or inhibit the growth of harmful organisms.

germ *noun* a disease-producing microorganism.

Proverbs Related to the Text

- Every man is a king in his own house.
- Chastise the good and he will mend.

Listen and Fill in the Blanks.

No, No, No.

Listen, all of you!

________ ______ ______ take direction.

________ ________ ______ have discipline.

________ ______ ______ have respect for your director.

I _________ slug you.

Ugh! I've been kissed by a dog.

I have dog germs!

Get hot water!

Get some disinfectant.

Get some iodine.

Ah!

Pronunciation Bites

한국인 영어발음오류유형 10 : 겹자음

글을 통한 영어학습을 주로 해온 한국인들이 흔히 범하는 오류 중의 하나가 철자상으로 겹자음으로 쓰여진 자음의 발음에서 나타난다. 현대영어에서 같은 자음이 두 번 반복되는 겹자음은 keenness, cleanness, unnecessary, unnoticed, unknowingly 와 같이 어간과 접사가 만나는 자리에서만 나타난다. 나머지 경우에는 자음이 하나만 있다고 발음하면 틀림없다. 한 가지 의문은 영어의 철자상 겹자음 표시는 그렇다면 아무런 역할을 하지 못하는가 하는 것이다. 결론은 그렇지 않다는 것이다. 영어의 겹자음은 영어의 역사에서 적어도 고대영어 기간 (서기 5세기에서 11세기 까지)에는 철자와 마찬가지로 두 개의 동일한 자음이 연속된 발음 또는 장자음(long consonant)의 표시였다. 그러나 중세영어(11세기에서 15세기까지)를 거쳐 현대영어에 이르는 동안에 역할의 변화가 생긴다. 영어에서 단어의 중간에 자음이 하나 이상 연속될 때 선행모음이 단모음 (short vowel)인 경우가 대부분 (chamber, matrix, apron 등은 제외)이므로 겹자음 표시도 이에 맞추어 선행모음이 단모음임을 표시하는 역할을 수행하는 것으로 되었다. 따라서 현대영어에서는 예외없이 겹자음 표시 앞의 모음은 단모음으로 실현된다. 본래 단어의 철자가 겹자음으로 된 경우 뿐 만 아니라 occur/occurred/occurrence, refer/referred/referral/등으로 겹자음으로 과거형, 명사형을 나타낸다. 그렇다면 open/opened, refer/reference에서는 왜 겹자음을 쓰지 않나? 그것은 겹자음 표시는 강세가 있는 음절에만 할 필요가 있기 때문이다. 이유는 영어에서 비강세음절은 저절로 축소모음이 되므로 비상세음설 뒤 자음을 겹자음으로 표기하지 않더라도 모음은 축소모음으로 실현되기 때문이다. 이러한 사실을 제대로 파악하지 못한 사람들이 영어 모국어 화자들에게도 있기 때문에 가끔 강세와 관계없이 level/levelled로 표기하는 경우가 나타난다.

Pronunciation Excercise

a. thinner, common, summer, ammonia

b. hotter, hitter, occurred, occurrence

c. bottom, battle, capped, tell, ball, topping, topped

Try it in English

1. 좀 맞아야 되겠어.

   I ought to __________ you

2. 교육 좀 받아야 되겠어.

   You've _______ _______ __________ discipline.

For Improvement of Your Critical Thinking

Question: Instead of humans, animal characters like dogs and cats are quite common in Western animation or comic strips. On the contrary, we Korean society rarely places animals as the main characters in novel or films. Describe the differences between Western and Asian culture in terms of animal characters in the showbiz industry.

Snoopy

Snoopy is a fictional character in the long-running comic strip *Peanuts*, by Charles M. Schulz. He is Charlie Brown's pet beagle. Snoopy began his life in the strip as a fairly ordinary dog, but eventually evolved into perhaps the strip's most dynamic character — and among the most recognizable comic characters in the world. The original drawings of Snoopy were based on Schulz's childhood dogs, Snooky and Spike. Snoopy, whose fictional birthday has been established as October 2, made his first appearance on the strip October 4, 1950, two days after the strip premiered. He was first identified by name on November 10. Schulz was originally going to call him "Sniffy" (as described in 25th anniversary book), until he discovered that name was used in a different comic strip. He changed it to "Snoopy" after remembering that his late mother Dena Schulz had commented that if their family were ever to acquire a third dog, it should be called Snoopi.

In earlier strips it is not clear who Snoopy belongs to; for instance in the February 2, 1951 strip, Charlie Brown accuses Snoopy of following him, only to be told by Patty that Snoopy isn't following Charlie Brown but merely lives in the same direction.[3] Indeed many early strips show Snoopy interacting with Shermy (who is shown in one early strip running with Snoopy on his leash) and Patty without Charlie Brown, making Snoopy appear to belong to all of the neighborhood kids, similar to the dog Pete in the Our Gang comedies, who is everyone's dog.

Snoopy was a silent character for the first two years of his existence, but on May 27, 1952 he verbalized his thoughts to readers for the first time via a thought balloon; Schulz would utilize this device for nearly all of the character's appearances in the strip thereafter. In addition to Snoopy's ability to "speak" his thoughts to the reader, many of the human characters in Peanuts have the uncanny knack of reading his thoughts and responding to them. In the animated Peanuts films and television specials, Snoopy's thoughts are not verbalized; his moods are instead conveyed through growls, sobs, laughter, etc., as well as through pantomime and foreign languages. The only exceptions are in *You're a Good Man, Charlie Brown* and *Snoopy!!! The Musical,* in which Snoopy's thoughts are verbalized through voiceovers (by Robert Towers and Cam Clarke, respectively). Animation producer Bill Meléndez voiced both Snoopy and (eventually) Woodstock in numerous television specials from 1965 to 2006. He does however shout "HEY!" in It's the Easter Beagle, Charlie Brown before dancing with some rabbits. (http://www.wikipedia.org)

11 Savant Syndrome

http://www.youtube.com/watch?v=YuhTFsiEcMU

This transcript is a round of questions and answers between two men: the interviewer is a psychology professor (abbreviated as P hereafter) and the interviewee is a boy conceived as having a savant syndrome (abbreviated as S hereafter).

(http://en.wikipedia.org/wiki/Rain_Man)

P: I'm gonna ask you some questions in years ahead.

S: Yeah.

P: All right. Ah, July 19 in the year 6,870, what day is that?

S: July 19, 6,870? That will be on a Saturday.

P: What do you say?

S: That'll be on a "Saturday."

P: All right. July 19 in the year 9,440.

S: July 19, 9440? That will be on a, that will be on a Sunday.

On a Sunday. *(the third man's voice)*

P: All right. We're going to check these dates later on. July 19 in the year 92,000-

July 19, 92,000-860.

S: 92,860. That will be — 92,860, July 19?

P: Right, July 19.

S: That will be on a, that will be on — July 9, 92,860 — that will be on a Monday.

On a Monday. *(the third man's voice)*

P: On a Monday? All right.

P: Now, July 19 in the year 132,470. Figure this one out!!

S: July 19? That would be on a Saturday.

P: Saturday? All right.

▪ ▪ ▪ ▪ ▪ ▪

P: Now, um, I want to ask some other questions.

S: Yeah!

P: How many days in a year?

S: 365.

S: 365.

P: Is it more than 365, or exactly 365?

S: In a leap year it's 366.

P: 366?

S: Leap year

P: All right. How many days in a week?

S: Seven.

P: How many months in a year?

S: Twelve.

P: How many hours in a day?

S: Twenty-four.

▪ ▪ ▪ ▪ ▪ ▪

P: How many minutes in an hour?

S: Ten minutes.

Ten minutes.

P: How many seconds in a minute?

S: Ten seconds.

P: Ten seconds? You sure it's not more than ten?

S: I am sure.

P: Sure? All right. How much is four times seven?

P: Four times seven?

S: I don't know.

P: You don't know? Come on, McBride taught you for months. You remember when McBride taught you?

S: Yeah.

P: What day was that he taught you on?

S: That was in 1964.

64

P: What month?

S: In February.

P: What ward?

S: Ward 5.

P: Right. Now, four times seven is how much?

S: Is it, uh, 21?.

P: 21. Couldn't it be more?

P: How much is 14 and 11?

S: 14 and 11 is 25.

P: How much is — if you buy a shirt-

S: Yeah.

P: And you go in a store and a shirt costs 4 dollars, and you give the man 10 dollar bill, how much change do you get back?

S: I don't know how much change.

P: Tell me, how much do you get back?

S: 20 cents.

Key Words & Expressions

figure out *phrasal verb* to understand with some difficulty: *No one can figure out why the plane crashed.*

leap year *noun* In the Gregorian calendar, a year that contains 366 days, with February 29 as an additional day: occurring in years whose last two digits are evenly divisible by four, except for centenary years not divisible by 400.

ward *noun* a division, floor, or room of a hospital for a particular class or group of patients: *a convalescent ward, a critical ward.*

cost *verb* to require the payment of money or something else of value in an exchange: *Careless driving costs lives.*

Proverbs Related to the Text

- Sickness shows what we are.
- He that wants health wants all.

Listen and Fill in the Blanks.

P: You don't know? Come on, McBride taught you for ___________. You remember when McBride taught you?

S: Yeah.

P: What day was that he taught ________ _______?

S: That was in 1964.

64

P: What month?

S: In February.

P: What ________?

S: ________ 5.

P: Right. Now, four ___________ seven is how much?

S: Is it, uh, 21?.

P: 21. Couldn't it be __________?

P: How much is 14 and 11?

S: 14 ________ 11 is 25.

P: How much is - if you buy a shirt-

S: Yeah.

P: And you _____ _____ a store and a shirt costs 4 dollars, and you give the man 10 dollar bill, how much change do you ______ ________?

S: I don't know how much change.

P: Tell me, how much do you get back?

S: _______ ________.

Pronunciation Bites

한국인 영어발음오류유형 11: 리듬

Pike, Abercrombie 등이 1940년대에 주장한 이래 리듬 (rhythm)의 면에서 세계언어는 두 가지 유형으로 나뉜다. 영국이나 미국영어, 독일어, 러시아어, 체코어 등은 '강세'(stress)가 리듬의 유지에 큰 역할을 하는 반면 한국어, 불어, 스페인어, 인도, 싱가폴, 필리핀, 자메이카 영어 등은 리듬을 강세보다는 '음절' 수에 의존하는 경향이 있다. 여기서 주목할 점은 한국어는 영국이나 미국영어의 강세의존 리듬이 아닌 음절 수에 의존한 리듬을 유지한다는 점이다. 따라서 한국어 모국어 화자는 영어를 읽거나 말할 때 한국어의 음절 수에 의존한 발음을 하여 리듬의 면에서 문제가 될 수 있다. 다음 문장 Which is the train to Busan, please?에서 본래 영어에서의 리듬과 한국인들의 리듬의 차이를 비교해 보자:

a. 영국과 미국영어의 리듬: (Which is the) (train to) (Busan) (please)?

b. 한국인 화자의 리듬: (Which is) (the train) (to Busan) (please)?

괄호로 묶은 리듬의 단위를 보면 영어는 음절의 수가 중요한 것이 아니라 강세가 중요하여 각각의 괄호 속에는 강세가 있는 음절이 하나씩 만 있다. 즉 which, train, Busan, please에 강세가 있고 나머지 단어들은 강세가 없을 뿐 더러 길이나 소리의 크기도 쪼그라들어 마치 강세가 있는 음절에 더부살이하는 신세처럼 발음된다. 반면에 (b)의 한국어 화자의 경우는 모든 음절이 대등한 위치에 있고 두 개의 음절씩 묶여 리듬의 단위를 형성하고 있다. 이렇게 되면 영어의 발음은 스타카토 (staccato)식이 되어 유려하지 못하고 딱딱 끊어지는 듯한 인상을 주게 된다. 논란이 있기는 하나 아시아 지역의 제2언어 (Second Language)로서의 영어, 예컨대 인도, 싱가포르, 필리핀 영어는 음절수에 의존한 리듬의 경향이 농후하다는 주장이 우세하고 있다. 이 지역에서 영어를 배울 경우 이 점을 주의할 필요가 있다.

Pronunciation Excercise

- The acorns of the oak are rolling down the street.
- All my clothes are hanging on the line.
- Chinese is spoken as a native language there.

Try it in English

1. 윤년은 4년에 한번 돌아온다.

   Every four years we a __________ _______________.

2. 매년 이 맘때면 낙엽이 진다.

   ________ ______ _____ ________, trees shed leaves.

For Improvement of Your Critical Thinking

Question: What is most likely to cause the disorders of savant syndromes, which are people who are uniquely outstanding in some area but extraordinarily incompetent in the other areas?

Savant

Kim Peek. Photo courtesy Darold A. Treffert, M.D. and the Wisconsin Medical Society

Savant syndrome, sometimes abbreviated as savantism, is not a recognized medical diagnosis, but researcher Darold Treffert defines it as a rare condition in which persons with developmental disorders (including autism spectrum disorders) have one or more areas of expertise, ability or brilliance that are in contrast with the individual's overall limitations. Treffert says the condition can be genetic, but can also be acquired. According to Treffert, about half of persons with savant syndrome have autistic disorder, while the other half have another developmental disability, mental retardation, brain injury or disease. He says, "... not all autistic persons have savant syndrome and not all persons with savant syndrome have autistic disorder". Other researchers state that autistic traits and savant skills may be linked, or have challenged some earlier conclusions about savant syndrome as "hearsay, uncorroborated by independent scrutiny". Though it is even more rare than the savant condition itself, some savants have no apparent abnormalities other than their unique abilities. This does not mean that these abilities weren't triggered by a brain injury of some sort but does temper the theory that all savants are disabled and that some sort of trade-off is required (http://www.wikipedia.org)

12 Zombies In Plain English

www.youtube.com/watch?v=bVnfyradCPY&feature=fvst

People dressed as zombies for Halloween, holding glasses of beer at a pub in Brighton originally posted to Flickr as Bar zombies. Author: Jeremy Keith

These days you have to watch your back. Danger may be lurking where you least expect it. You may find a relative, friend or neighbor coming after one thing — your brain.

This Halloween is forecasted to be a high season for zombie attacks, and we're going to help you get through it, brain intact.

This is Zombies in Plain English.

The first step is identifying a zombie.

Let's take your uncle Dan. Here is Dan as we all know him, a normal guy. Now let's look at Dan as a zombie.

Notice the unnatural mouth position and dark eyes. The shoulders will be off kilter, arms reaching, grabbing; legs limpy; skin pale. This is a zombie.

Be careful this Halloween. You may see people that resemble zombies. Remember: Zombies don't eat candy - only brains.

You may also see them dancing with Michael Jackson. These are actors. Zombies don't dance.

When you encounter on a real zombie, it's time to have a plan. Here is how to survive an attack. Your first reaction may be to retreat to a home or business. This is only a short-term solution because they will never stop, ever. Instead, consider heading to a Costco.

Don't plan to wait out an attack without proper rations. Now keep your cool. Remember that zombies may move quickly in the early stages of infection. Don't underestimate their speed. Also, consider a retreat to high altitudes. Studies have shown that zombies react poorly to cold weather, causing them to become brittle and slow.

Lastly zombies can't swim. So retreat via boat could help. And remember those rations.

If you're not the retreating type, the obvious next move is counter-attack. This brings us to our last step: how to kill the undead.

The simple idea is: kill the brain, stop the zombie. This is generally done through head trauma or decapitation, but any method that removes the zombie brain's ability to direct the undead body will work.

As starting points, we suggest large caliber bullets to the head or decapitation via machete, axe or chain saw. Now, chain saws are advanced tools that should be used carefully.

Napalm or grenades can also be effective. But be careful. A flaming zombie can be even more dangerous than a normal one.

If your friend has a zombie bite, unfortunately there is only one outcome. Infection is absolutely irreversible. Don't bother with antiseptic or Band-Aids. Your friend is not your friend any more. Face the inevitable, and save your brain.

Kill them with dignity before they become undead too. Remember, be prepared. Plan your root and rations. Be on the look-out, and when they -

Whoa, this just in. We've received an unconfirmed report that zombies have been sighted inside Southern British Columbia. They may be heading south. Repeat. Heading south.

Sachi! What the ... ? Did you hear that? Uh – eh...

The question is: are you prepared? Have a fun, safe and zombie-free Halloween. From your friends at Commoncraft.

Key Words & Expressions

kilter *noun* good condition: *The plane was out of kilter.*

limp *verb* to walk with a labored, jerky movement, as when lame.

retreat *verb* to withdraw, retire, or draw back, for shelter or seclusion.

trauma *noun* a body wound or shock produced by sudden physical injury, as from violence or accident.

chain saw *noun* a power saw, usually portable, having teeth set on an endless chain.

decapitate *verb* to cut off the head of, behead: *Many people were decapitated during the Korean War.*

irreversible *adjective* not reversible; incapable of being changed.

Proverbs Related to the Text

- A friend in need is a friend indeed.
- One father can support ten children; ten children cannot support one father.
- Love makes the world go around.

Listen and Fill in the Blanks.

When you encounter on a real zombie, it's time to have a plan. Here is how to survive an attack. Your first reaction may be to _________ to a home or business. This is only a short-term solution because they will never stop, ever. Instead, consider heading to a Costco.

Don't plan to wait out an attack without proper rations. Now keep your cool. Remember that zombies may move quickly in the early stages of infection. Don't underestimate their speed. Also, consider a retreat to high __________. Studies have shown that zombies react poorly to cold weather, causing them to become brittle and slow.
Lastly zombies can't swim. So retreat via boat could help. And remember those _________.

If you're not the retreating type, the obvious next move is counter-attack. This brings us to our last step: how to kill undead.

The simple idea is: kill the brain, stop the zombie. This is generally done through head _________ or ___________, but any method that removes the zombie brain's ability to direct the undead body will work.

As starting points, we suggest large _________ _________ to the head or decapitation _______ machete, axe or chain saw. Now, chain saws are advanced tools that should be used carefully.

Napalm or _________ can also be effective. But be careful. A flaming zombie can be even more dangerous than a normal one.

Pronunciation Bites

한국인 영어발음오류유형 12 : [θ, ð, f, v, r, l]

한국인들의 영어발음 오류에는 한국어에 존재하지 않은 영어 말소리의 경우 영어에 가장 가까운 한국어 말소리로 대체하게 된다. 독일인, 프랑스 영어의 thin [θ]을 /s/으로 then /ðen/을 [zen]으로 발음하는 이유는 이 소리는 자국어에는 존재하지 않아 나름대로 가장 근접한 소리를 낸 결과이다. 중국인들은 보통 이들을 각각 thin [fin], then [zen]으로 발음한다. 그러면 한국어에 존재하지 않는 영어 말소리들을 한국인들이 흔히 어떻게 발음하는지 보자. 영어의 치간마찰음 (interdental fricative) /θ/는 [s'] ([ㅆ])으로, /ð/는 [t]([ㄷ])으로 대체한다.

thin → [s'in]
then → [ten]

영어의 양순 마찰음 (bilabial fricative) /v/는 [p]로 대체되어 영어의 /b/와 동일하게 실현시킨다.

verry/ berry/bury → [peri]

중국, 한국, 일본의 극동 3국어가 공통적으로 /r/과 /l/을 구분하지 않으며 어두에서는 한국인들은 보통 /r/로 발음한다.

river/liver → [ribə]

이러한 발음 오류는 영어 마찰음의 조음위치, 조음방식, /r/과 /l/의 조음방식에 대한 훈련을 해야 제대로 소리를 낼 수 있다. 여기서는 마찰음(θ, ð, f, v)은 아랫입술, 혀가 윗입술, 입천장에 닿지 않는다는 점과 /l/은 /r/과는 달리 혀끝이 잇몸에 닿은 상태에서 조음된다는 점만 유념하여 다음을 연습하기로 하자.

Pronunciation Excercise

think, thank, bath, McCarthy, path
then, there, they, the, though, bathe
vocal, victor, victim, vindicate, advance
raw, river, rise, royal, rotate, porter
low, level, legal, sill, liver, land, allege

Try it in English

1. 그는 차동차 사고로 가사상태에 빠졌다.

   The car crash drove him to a state of ________ ________.

2. 영혼이 떠난 육체가 과연 존재할까?

   Is there, if any, a physical body _______ _________?

3. 죽음에 대한 불안감은 현대인들도 마찬가지다.

   It is also true that any person of today has _______ to the matter of death.

For Improvement of Your Critical Thinking

Question: Zombies are one of the themes frequently employed in modern cultural genres like films, fictions and computer games. The name or concept of zombie computer makes us more familiar with zombies, which have deep connection to Caribbean or African religious customs. Here is the question: What would stimulate us to be haunted by the horrible entity of the "living dead"?

Zombie

A zombie is a creature that appears in folklore and popular culture typically as a reanimated corpse or a mindless human being. Stories of zombies originated in the Afro-Caribbean spiritual belief system of Vodou, which told of the people being controlled as laborers by a powerful sorcerer. Zombies became a popular device in modern horror fiction, largely because of the success of George A. Romero's 1968 film *Night of the Living Dead.*

There are several possible etymologies of the word zombie. One possible origin is jumbie, the West Indian term for "ghost". Another is nzambi, the Kongo word meaning "spirit of a dead person." According to the Merriam-Webster dictionary, the word entered English circa 1871 and is derived from the Louisiana Creole or Haitian Creole zonbi, which in turn is of Bantu origin. A zonbi is a person who is believed to have died and been brought back to life without speech or free will. It is akin to the Kimbundu nzúmbe ghost.

Modern zombies, as portrayed in books, films, games, and haunted attractions, are different from both voodoo zombies and those of folklore. Modern zombies are typically depicted in popular culture as mindless, unfeeling monsters with a hunger for human flesh, a prototype established in the seminal 1968 film *Night of the Living Dead.* Typically, these creatures can sustain damage far beyond that of a normal, living human. Generally these can only be killed by a wound to the head, such as a headshot, and can pass whatever syndrome that causes their condition onto others.

A zombie computer (often shortened as zombie) is a computer attached to the Internet that has been compromised by a hacker, a computer virus, or a trojan horse. Generally, a compromised machine is only one of many in a botnet, and will be used to perform malicious tasks of one sort or another under remote direction. Most owners of zombie computers are unaware that their system is being used in this way. Because the owner tends to be unaware, these computers are metaphorically compared to zombies.

Zombies have been used extensively to send e-mail spam; as of 2005, an estimated 50–80% of all spam worldwide was sent by zombie computers. This allows spammers to avoid detection and presumably reduces their bandwidth costs, since the owners of zombies pay for their own bandwidth. This spam also greatly furthers the spread of Trojan horses; as Trojans, unlike viruses are not self-replicating, unlike worms, they rely on the movement of e-mails or spam to grow. (http//:www.wikipedia.org)

13 Presidential Inauguration
Speech by Dwight Eisenhower at the 1st Inauguration, 1953

http://www.americanrhetoric.com/speeches/dwighteisenhowerfirstinaugural.htm

From http://en.wikipedia.org/wiki/World_War_II

My friends, before I begin the expression of those thoughts that I deem appropriate to this moment, would you permit me the privilege of uttering a little private prayer of my own? And I ask that you bow your heads:

Almighty God, as we stand here at this moment my associates – my future associates in the Executive branch of Government join me in beseeching that Thou will make full and complete our dedication to the service of the people in this throng, and their fellow citizens everywhere. Give us, we pray, the power to discern clearly right from wrong, and allow all our words and actions to be governed thereby, and by the laws of this land. Especially we pray that our concern shall be for all the people regardless of station, race, or calling. May cooperation be permitted and be the mutual aim of those who, under the concepts of our Constitution, hold to differing political faiths; so that all may work for the good of our beloved country and Thy glory. Amen.

My fellow citizens:

The world and we have passed the midway point of a century of continuing challenge. We sense with all our faculties that forces of good and evil are massed and armed and opposed as rarely before in history.

This fact defines the meaning of this day. We are summoned by this honored and historic ceremony to witness more than the act of one citizen swearing his oath of service, in the presence of his God. We are called as a people to give testimony in the sight of the world to our faith that the future shall belong to the free.

Since this century's beginning, a time of tempest has seemed to come upon the continents of the earth. Masses of Asia have awakened to strike off shackles of the past. Great nations of Europe have fought their bloodiest wars. Thrones have toppled and their vast – vast empires have disappeared. New nations have been born.

For our own country, it has been a time of recurring trial. We have grown in power and in responsibility. We have passed through the anxieties of depression and of war, but to a summit unmatched in man's history. Seeking to secure peace in the world, while we have had to fight our way through the forests of the Argonne to the shores of Iwo Jima, and to the cold mountains of Korea.

In the swift rush of great events, we find ourselves groping to know the full sense and meaning of these times in which we live. In our quest of understanding, we beseech God's guidance. We summon all our knowledge of the past and we scan all signs of the future. We bring all our wit and all our will to meet the question: How far have we come in man's long pilgrimage from darkness toward the light? Are we nearing the light – a day of freedom and of peace for all mankind? Or are the shadows of another night closing in upon us?

Great as are the preoccupations absorbing us at home, concerned as we are with matters that deeply affect our livelihood today and our vision of the future, each of these domestic problems is dwarfed by, and often even created by, this question that involves all humankind.

This trial comes at a moment when man's power to achieve good or to inflict evil surpasses the brightest hopes and the sharpest fears of all ages. We can turn rivers in their courses, level mountains to the plains. Oceans and land and sky are avenues for our colossal commerce. Disease diminishes and life lengthens.

Yet the promise of this life is imperiled by the very genius that has made it possible. Nations amass wealth. Labor sweats to create – and turns out devices to level not only mountains but also cities. Science seems ready to confer upon us, as its final gift, the power to erase human life from this planet.

At such a time in history, we who are free must proclaim anew our faith. This faith is the abiding creed of our fathers. It is our faith in the deathless dignity of man, as governed by eternal moral and natural laws.

This faith defines our full view of life. It establishes, beyond debate, those gifts of the Creator that are man's inalienable rights, and that make all men equal in His sight.

In the light of this equality, we know that the virtues most cherished by free people – love of truth, pride of work, devotion to country – all are treasures equally precious in the lives of the most humble and of the most exalted. The men who mine coal and fire furnaces, and balance ledgers, and turn lathes, and pick cotton, and heal the sick and plant corn – all serve as proudly and as profitably for America as the statesmen who draft treaties and the legislators who enact laws.

This faith rules our whole way of life. It decrees that we, the people, elect leaders not to rule but to serve. It asserts that we have the right to choice of our own work and to the reward of our own toil. It inspires the initiative that makes our productivity the wonder of the world. And it warns that any man who seeks to deny equality among all his brothers betrays the spirit of the free and invites the mockery of the tyrant.

It is because we, all of us, hold to these principles that the political changes accomplished this day do not imply turbulence, upheaval, or disorder. Rather, this change expresses a purpose of strengthening our dedication and devotion to the precepts of our founding documents, a conscious renewal of faith in our country and in the watchfulness of a Divine Providence. The enemies of this faith know no god but force, no devotion but its use. They tutor men in treason. They feed upon the hunger of others. Whatever defies them, they torture, especially the truth.

Here, then, is joined no argument between slightly different philosophies. This conflict strikes directly at the faith of our fathers and at the lives of our sons. No principle or treasure that we hold, from the spiritual knowledge of our free schools and churches to the creative magic of free labor and capital, nothing lies safely beyond the reach of this struggle. Freedom is pitted against slavery; lightness against the dark.

The faith we hold belongs not to us alone but to the free of all the world. This common bond binds the grower of rice in Burma and the planter of wheat in Iowa, the shepherd in southern Italy and the mountaineer in the Andes. It confers a common dignity upon the French soldier who dies in Indo-China, the British soldier killed in Malaya, the American life given in Korea.

We know, beyond this, that we are linked to all free peoples not merely by a noble idea but by a simple need. No free people can for long cling to any privilege or enjoy any safety in economic solitude. For all our own material might, even we need markets in the world for the surpluses of our farms and our factories. Equally, we need for these same farms and factories vital materials and products of distant lands. This basic law of interdependence, so manifest in the commerce of peace, applies with thousand-fold intensity in the event of war.

So are we persuaded by necessity and by belief that the strength of all free peoples lies in unity; their danger, in discord. To produce this unity, to meet the challenge of our time, destiny has laid upon our country the responsibility of the free world's leadership. So it is proper that we assure our friends once again that, in the discharge of this responsibility, we Americans know and we observe the difference between world leadership and imperialism; between firmness and truculence; between a thoughtfully calculated goal and spasmodic reaction to the stimulus of emergencies. We wish our friends the world over to know this above all: we face the threat, not with dread and confusion, but with confidence and conviction.

We feel this moral strength because we know that we are not helpless prisoners of history. We are free men. We shall remain free, never to be proven guilty of the one capital offense against freedom, a lack of staunch faith.

In pleading our just cause before the bar of history and in pressing our – and in pressing our labor for world peace, we shall be guided by certain fixed principles. These principles are:

Number 1: Abhorring war as a chosen way to balk the purposes of those who threaten us, we hold it to be the first task of statesmanship to develop the strength that will deter the forces of aggression and promote the conditions of peace. For, as it must be the supreme purpose of all free men, so it must be the dedication of their leaders, to save humanity from preying upon itself.

In the light of this principle, we stand ready to engage with any and all others in joint effort to remove the causes of mutual fear and distrust among nations, so as to make possible drastic reduction of armaments. The sole requisites for undertaking such effort are that, in their purpose, they be aimed logically and honestly toward secure peace for all; and that, in their result, they provide methods by which every participating nation will prove good faith in carrying out its pledge.

Number 2: Realizing that common sense and common decency alike dictate the futility of appeasement, we shall never try to placate an aggressor by the false and wicked bargain of trading honor for security. Americans, indeed, all free men, remember that in the final choice a soldier's pack is not so heavy a burden as a prisoner's chains.

Number 3: Knowing that only a United States that is strong and immensely productive can help defend freedom in our world, we view our nation's strength and security as a trust upon which rests the hope of free men everywhere. It is the firm duty of each of our free citizens and of every free citizen everywhere to place the cause of his country before the comfort, the convenience of himself.

And number 4: Honoring the identity and the special heritage of each nation in the world, we shall never use our strength to try to impress upon another people our own cherished political and economic institutions.

Number 5: Assessing realistically the needs and capacities of proven friends of freedom, we shall strive to help them to achieve their own security and well-being. Likewise, we shall count upon them to assume, within the limits of their resources, their full and just burdens in the common defense of freedom.

Number 6: Recognizing economic health as an indispensable basis of military strength and the free world's peace, we shall strive to foster everywhere, and to practice ourselves, policies that encourage productivity and profitable trade. For the impoverishment of any single people in the world means danger to the well-being of all other peoples.

Number 7: Appreciating that economic need, military security, and political wisdom combine to suggest regional groupings of free peoples, we hope, within the framework of the United Nations, to help strengthen such special bonds the world over. The nature of these ties must vary with the different problems of different areas. In the Western Hemisphere, we enthusiastically join with all our neighbors in the work of perfecting a community of fraternal trust and common purpose. In Europe, we ask that enlightened and inspired leaders of the Western nations strive with renewed vigor to make the unity of their peoples a reality. Only as free Europe unitedly marshals its strength can it effectively safeguard, even with our help, its spiritual and cultural heritage.

Number 8: Conceiving the defense of freedom, like freedom itself, to be one and indivisible, we hold all continents and peoples in equal regard and honor. We reject any insinuation that one race or another, one people or another, is in any sense inferior or expendable.

Number 9: Respecting the United Nations as the living sign of all people's hope for peace, we shall strive to make it not merely an eloquent symbol but an effective force. And in our quest for an honorable peace, we shall neither compromise, nor tire, nor ever cease.

By these rules of conduct, we hope to be known to all peoples.

By their observance, an earth of peace may become not a vision but a fact.

This hope, this supreme aspiration, must rule the way we live.

We must be ready to dare all for our country. For history does not long entrust the care of freedom to the weak or the timid. We must acquire proficiency in defense and display stamina in purpose.

We must be willing, individually and as a Nation, to accept whatever sacrifices may be required of us. A people that values its privileges above its principles soon loses both.

These basic precepts are not lofty abstractions, far removed from matters of daily living. They are laws of spiritual strength that generate and define our material strength. Patriotism means equipped forces and a prepared citizen[ry]. Moral stamina means more energy and more productivity, on the farm and in the factory. Love of liberty means the guarding of every resource that makes freedom possible – from the sanctity of our families and the wealth of our soil to the genius of our scientists.

And so each citizen plays an indispensable role. The productivity of our heads, our hands, and our hearts is the source of all the strength we can command, for both the enrichment of our lives and the winning of the peace.

No person, no home, no community can be beyond the reach of this call. We are summoned to act in wisdom and in conscience, to work with industry, to teach with persuasion, to preach with conviction, to weigh our every deed with care and with compassion. For this truth must be clear before us: whatever America hopes to bring to pass in the world must first come to pass in the heart of America.

The peace we seek, then, is nothing less than the practice and the fulfillment of our whole faith among ourselves and in our dealings with others. This signifies more than the stilling of guns, easing the sorrow of war. More than escape from death, it is a way of life. More than a haven for the weary, it is a hope for the brave.

This is the hope that beckons us onward in this century of trial. This is the work that awaits us all, to be done with bravery, with charity, and with prayer to Almighty God.

My citizens — I thank you.

Key Words & Expressions

beseech *verb* to make urgent appeal: *Seriously did I beseech, but to no avail.*

throng *noun* a multitude of people crowded or assembled together, crowd.

midway *noun* a place or part situated midway.

tempest *noun* a violent windstorm, one with rain, hail, or snow.

Argonne The Forest of Argonne forms a long strip of rocky mountain and wild woodland in north-eastern France. The forest is also the site of military action during World War I. Several United States Army soldiers earned the Medal of Honor there, including Colonel Nelson Miles Holderman, Major Charles White Whittlesey, and Sergeant Alvin C. York. (http://www.wikipedia.org)

Iwo Jima The Battle of Iwo Jima (February 19~March 26, 1945), or Operation Detachment, was a battle in which the United States fought for and captured Iwo Jima (lit. Iwo Island) from Japan. The battle produced some of the fiercest fighting in the Pacific Campaign of World War II. (http://www.wikipedia.org)

dwarf *verb* to cause to appear or seem small in size, extent, character etc.: *He dwarfed his opponent in athletic skill.*

colossal *adjective* extraordinarily great in size, extent, or degree, gigantic, huge.

abiding *adjective* continuing without change, enduring: *an abiding faith.*

ledger *noun* a flat slab of stone placed over a grave or tomb.

lathe *noun* a machine for use in working wood, metal, etc., that holds the material and rotates it about a horizontal axis against a tool that shapes it.

Divine Providence Traditional theism holds that God is the creator of heaven and earth, and that all that occurs in the universe takes place under Divine Providence — that is, under God's sovereign guidance and control.

pit against *phrasal verb* Set in direct opposition or competition: *The Korean War pitted brother against brother.*

truculence *noun* being aggressively hostile, belligerent.

balk *verb* to place an obstacle in the way of, hinder: *the sudden upheaval balked her hopes.*

prey *verb* to victimize another or others: *huge sharks that prey upon the poor.*

marshal *verb* to arrange in proper order, set out in an orderly manner.

safeguard *verb* to guard, protect, secure.

beckon *verb* to signal, summon, or direct by a gesture of the head or hand.

Provebs Related to the Text

- Pardoning the bad is injuring the good.
- Patience is bitter, but its fruit is sweet.
- You can't please everybody.

Listen and Fill in the Blanks.

Almighty God, as we stand here at this moment my ___________– my future associates in the Executive branch of Government ________ _____ in beseeching that Thou will make full and complete our dedication to the ___________ of the people in this _________, and their fellow citizens everywhere. Give us, we pray, the power to ___________ clearly right from wrong, and allow all our ________ and _________ to be governed __________, and by the laws of this land. Especially we pray that our concern shall be for all the people regardless of station, race, or _________. May cooperation be permitted and be the mutual aim of those who, under the concepts of our Constitution, _______ to differing political faiths; so that all may work for the __________ of our __________ country and Thy glory. Amen.

Pronunciation Bites

한국인 영어발음오류유형 13 : 기능어의 발음

다음 문장에서 기울임체로 표시된 that은 같은 형태로 발음되지 않는다.

That is the stuff *that* I am looking for.

첫 번째 that은 지시대명사로서 단어강세가 부여되는 반면 두 번째 that은 관계대명사로서 단어강세가 주어지지 않는다. 강세만이 아니다. 첫 번째 that은 /ðæt/인 반면 두 번째 that은 /ðət/ 으로 발음될 것이다. 다른 유형의 한국인 발음오류에서 지적한 바와 같이 강세 유무에 따라 단어의 발음의 근본적인 변화가 있게 된다. 강세를 가진 단어 즉 내용어(content word)와 강세가 부재한 단어 즉 기능어(function word)를 구분하지 않는 일반적인 오류에서 벗어나야 영어다운 영어를 구사하게 된다. 이러한 강세가 기본적으로 주어지지 않는 단어라도 문장에 따라 강조강세(empathetic stress)나 대조강세(contrastive stress)를 받는 경우는 일반 단어와 마찬가지로 축소모음이나 자음이 탈락하는 현상이 방지된다. 다음의 경우를 연습해 보자

Pronunciation Excercise

	강세를 받는 경우	일반적인 경우
and	ænd	ənd, ən, n
them	ðem	ðəm, əm
as	æz	əz
the	ði	ðə, ði
a	ey	ə
of	ʌv	əv, ə
he	hiː	iː
because	bɪkɔːz	bɪkəz

Try it in English

1. 그의 변함없는 신념은 믿음직스럽다.

   You can trust his __________ __________.

2. 그 장사는 더 강한 장사와 싸워야 했다.

   The strong man had to _________ _________ the stronger man.

3. 비상상황이 발생해 그의 희망이 좌절되었다.

   The emergency _________ his hope.

For Improvement of Your Critical Thinking

Question: President Eisenhower started his inaugural speech by a Christian prayer. Obviously he knew not all Americans or other audiences would like his religious gesture. Like Korean society, America is not monolithic in terms of religion. Are you for or against the President's attitude in the super-formal ceremony?

Dwight Eisenhower

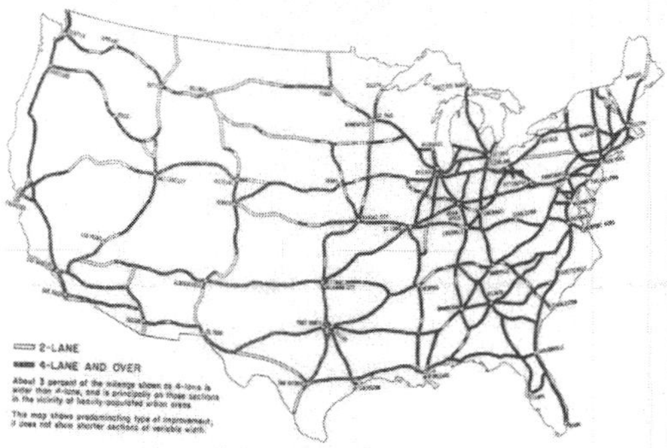

Figure 3.—Estimated status of improvement of the National System of Interstate Highways as to lane width, in 1965.

Dwight David "Ike" Eisenhower (October 14, 1890~March 28, 1969) was the 34th President of the United States from 1953 until 1961 and a five-star general in the United States Army. During the Second World War, he served as Supreme Commander of the Allied forces in Europe, with responsibility for planning and supervising the successful invasion of France and Germany in 1944~45. In 1951, he became the first supreme commander of NATO.

As President, he oversaw the cease-fire of the Korean War, kept up the pressure on the Soviet Union during the Cold War, made nuclear weapons a higher defense priority, launched the Space Race, enlarged the Social Security program, and began the Interstate Highway System as shown by the map above. He was the last World War I veteran to serve as U.S. president, and the last president born in the 19th century. Eisenhower ranks highly among former U.S. presidents in terms of approval rating.

www.wikipedia.org

14 Stanford University Commencement Speech 2008 by Oprah Winfrey

http://www.youtube.com/watch?v=Bpd3raj8xww

Thank you, President Hennessy, and to the trustees and the faculty, to all of the parents and grandparents, to you, the Stanford graduates. Thank you for letting me share this amazing day with you.

I need to begin by letting everyone in on a little secret. The secret is that Kirby Bumpus, Stanford Class of '08, is my goddaughter. So, I was thrilled when President Hennessy asked me to be your Commencement speaker, because this is the first time I've been allowed on campus since Kirby's been here.

You see, Kirby's a very smart girl. She wants people to get to know her on her own terms, she says. Not in terms of who she knows. So, she never wants anyone who's first meeting her to know that I know her and she knows me. So, when she first came to Stanford for new student orientation with her mom, I hear that they arrived and everybody was so welcoming, and somebody came up to Kirby and they said, "Ohmigod, that's Gayle King!" Because a lot of people know Gayle King as my BFF [best friend forever].

And so somebody comes up to Kirby, and they say, "Ohmigod, is that Gayle King?" And Kirby's like, "h-huh. She's my mom."

And so the person says, Ohmigod, does it mean, like, you know Oprah

Winfrey?"

And Kirby says, "Sort of."

I said, "Sort of? You sort of know me?" Well, I have photographic proof. I have pictures which I can e-mail to you all of Kirby riding horsey with me on all fours. So, I more than sort-of know Kirby Bumpus. And I'm so happy to be here, just happy that I finally, after four years, get to see her room. There's really nowhere else I'd rather be, because I'm so proud of Kirby, who graduates today with two degrees, one in human bio and the other in psychology. Love you, Kirby Cakes! That's how well I know her. I can call her Cakes.

And so proud of her mother and father, who helped her get through this time, and her brother, Will. I really had nothing to do with her graduating from Stanford, but every time anybody's asked me in the past couple of weeks what I was doing, I would say, "I'm getting ready to go to Stanford."

I just love saying "Stanford." Because the truth is, I know I would have never gotten my degree at all, 'cause I didn't go to Stanford. I went to Tennessee State University. But I never would have gotten my diploma at all, because I was supposed to graduate back in 1975, but I was short one credit. And I figured, I'm just going to forget it, 'cause, you know, I'm not going to march with my class. Because by that point, I was already on television. I'd been in television since I was 19 and a sophomore. Granted, I was the only television anchor person that had an 11 o'clock curfew doing the 10 o'clock news.

Seriously, my dad was like, "Well, that news is over at 10:30. Be home by 11."

But that didn't matter to me, because I was earning a living. I was on my way. So, I thought, I'm going to let this college thing go and I only had one credit short. But, my father, from that time on and for years after, was always on my case, because I did not graduate. He'd say, "Oprah Gail"—that's my middle name—"I don't know what you're gonna do without that degree." And I'd say, "But, Dad, I have my own television show."

And he'd say, "Well, I still don't know what you're going to do without that degree."

And I'd say, "But, Dad, now I'm a talk show host." He'd say, "I don't know how you're going to get another job without that degree."

So, in 1987, Tennessee State University invited me back to speak at their commencement. By then, I had my own show, was nationally syndicated. I'd made a movie, had been nominated for an Oscar and founded my company, Harpo. But I told them, I cannot come and give a speech unless I can earn one more credit, because my dad's still saying I'm not going to get anywhere without that degree.

So, I finished my coursework, I turned in my final paper and I got the degree.

And my dad was very proud. And I know that, if anything happens, that one credit will be my salvation.

But I also know why my dad was insisting on that diploma, because, as B. B. King put it, "The beautiful thing about learning is that nobody can take that away from you." And learning is really in the broadest sense what I want to talk about today, because your education, of course, isn't ending here. In many ways, it's only just begun.

The world has so many lessons to teach you. I consider the world, this Earth, to be like a school and our life the classrooms. And sometimes here in this Planet Earth school the lessons often come dressed up as detours or roadblocks. And sometimes as full-blown crises. And the secret I've learned to getting ahead is being open to the lessons, lessons from the grandest university of all, that is, the universe itself.

It's being able to walk through life eager and open to self-improvement and that which is going to best help you evolve, 'cause that's really why we're here, to evolve as human beings. To grow into more of ourselves, always moving to the next level of understanding, the next level of compassion and growth.

I think about one of the greatest compliments I've ever received: I interviewed with a reporter when I was first starting out in Chicago. And then many years later, I saw the same reporter. And she said to me, "You know what? You really haven't changed. You've just become more of yourself."

And that is really what we're all trying to do, become more of ourselves. And I believe that there's a lesson in almost everything that you do and every experience, and getting the lesson is how you move forward. It's how you enrich your spirit. And, trust me, I know that inner wisdom is more precious than wealth. The more you spend it, the more you gain.

So, today, I just want to share a few lessons—meaning three—that I've learned in my journey so far. And aren't you glad? Don't you hate it when somebody says, "I'm going to share a few," and it's 10 lessons later? And, you're like, "Listen, this is my graduation. This is not about you." So, it's only going to be three.

The three lessons that have had the greatest impact on my life have to do with feelings, with failure and with finding happiness.

A year after I left college, I was given the opportunity to co-anchor the 6 o'clock news in Baltimore, because the whole goal in the media at the time I was coming up was you try to move to larger markets. And Baltimore was a much larger market than Nashville. So, getting the 6 o'clock news co-anchor job at 22 was such a big deal. It felt like the biggest deal in the world at the time.

And I was so proud, because I was finally going to have my chance to be like Barbara Walters, which is who I had been trying to emulate since the start of my TV career. So, I was 22 years old, making $22,000 a year. And it's where I met my best friend, Gayle, who was an intern at the same TV station. And once we became friends, we'd say, "Ohmigod, I can't believe it! You're making $22,000 and you're only

22. Imagine when you're 40 and you're making $40,000!"

When I turned 40, I was so glad that didn't happen.

So, here I am, 22, making $22,000 a year and, yet, it didn't feel right. It didn't feel right. The first sign, as President Hennessy was saying, was when they tried to change my name. The news director said to me at the time, "Nobody's going to remember Oprah. So, we want to change your name. We've come up with a name we think that people will remember and people will like. It's a friendly name: Suzie."

Hi, Suzie. Very friendly. You can't be angry with Suzie. Remember Suzie. But my name wasn't Suzie. And, you know, I'd grown up not really loving my name, because when you're looking for your little name on the lunch boxes and the license plate tags, you're never going to find Oprah.

So, I grew up not loving the name, but once I was asked to change it, I thought, well, it is my name and do I look like a Suzie to you? So, I thought, no, it doesn't feel right. I'm not going to change my name. And if people remember it or not, that's OK.

And then they said they didn't like the way I looked. This was in 1976, when your boss could call you in and say, "I don't like the way you look." Now that would be called a lawsuit, but back then they could just say, "I don't like the way you look." Which, in case some of you in the back, if you can't tell, is nothing like Barbara Walters. So, they sent me to a salon where they gave me a perm, and after a few days all my hair fell out and I had to shave my head. And then they really didn't like the way I looked.

Because now I am black and bald and sitting on TV. Not a pretty picture.

But even worse than being bald, I really hated, hated, hated being sent to report on other people's tragedies as a part of my daily duty, knowing that I was just expected to observe, when everything in my instinct told me that I should be doing something, I should be lending a hand.

So, as President Hennessy said, I'd cover a fire and then I'd go back and I'd try to give the victims blankets. And I wouldn't be able to sleep at night because of all the things I was covering during the day.

And, meanwhile, I was trying to sit gracefully like Barbara and make myself talk like Barbara. And I thought, well, I could make a pretty goofy Barbara. And if I could figure out how to be myself, I could be a pretty good Oprah. I was trying to sound elegant like Barbara. And sometimes I didn't read my copy, because something inside me said, this should be spontaneous. So, I wanted to get the news as I was giving it to the people. So, sometimes, I wouldn't read my copy and it would be, like, six people on a pileup on I-40. Oh, my goodness.

And sometimes I wouldn't read the copy—because I wanted to be spontaneous—and I'd come across a list of words I didn't know and I'd mispronounce. And one day I was reading copy and I called Canada "ca nada." And I decided, this Barbara thing's not going too well. I should try being myself.

But at the same time, my dad was saying, "Oprah Gail, this is an opportunity of a lifetime. You better keep that job." And my boss was saying, "This is the nightly news. You're an anchor, not a social worker. Just do your job."

So, I was juggling these messages of expectation and obligation and feeling really miserable with myself. I'd go home at night and fill up my journals, 'cause I've kept a journal since I was 15—so I now have volumes of journals. So, I'd go home at night and fill up my journals about how miserable I was and frustrated. Then I'd eat my anxiety. That's where I learned that habit.

And after eight months, I lost that job. They said I was too emotional. I was too much. But since they didn't want to pay out the contract, they put me on a talk show in Baltimore. And the moment I sat down on that show, the moment I did, I felt like I'd come home. I realized that TV could be more than just a playground, but a platform for service, for helping other people lift their lives. And the moment I sat down, doing that talk show, it felt like breathing. It felt right. And that's where everything that followed for me began.

And I got that lesson. When you're doing the work you're meant to do, it feels right and every day is a bonus, regardless of what you're getting paid.

It's true. And how do you know when you're doing something right? How do you know that? It feels so. What I know now is that feelings are really your GPS system for life. When you're supposed to do something or not supposed to do something, your emotional guidance system lets you know. The trick is to learn to check your ego at the door and start checking your gut instead. Every right decision I've made—every right decision I've ever made—has come from my gut. And every wrong decision I've ever made was a result of me not listening to the greater voice of myself.

If it doesn't feel right, don't do it. That's the lesson. And that lesson alone will save you, my friends, a lot of grief. Even doubt means don't. This is what I've learned. There are many times when you don't know what to do. When you don't know what to do, get still, get very still, until you do know what to do.

And when you do get still and let your internal motivation be the driver, not only will your personal life improve, but you will gain a competitive edge in the working world as well. Because, as Daniel Pink writes in his best-seller, A Whole New Mind, we're entering a whole new age. And he calls it the Conceptual Age, where traits that set people apart today are going to come from our hearts—right brain—as well as our heads. It's no longer just the logical, linear, rules-based thinking that matters, he says. It's also empathy and joyfulness and purpose, inner traits that have transcendent worth.

These qualities bloom when we're doing what we love, when we're involving the wholeness of ourselves in our work, both our expertise and our emotion.

So, I say to you, forget about the fast lane. If you really want to fly, just harness your power to your passion. Honor your calling. Everybody has one. Trust your heart and success will come to you.

So, how do I define success? Let me tell you, money's pretty nice. I'm not going to stand up here and tell you that it's not about money, 'cause money is very nice. I like money. It's good for buying things.

But having a lot of money does not automatically make you a successful person. What you want is money and meaning. You want your work to be meaningful. Because meaning is what brings the real richness to your life. What you really want is to be surrounded by people you trust and treasure and by people who cherish you. That's when you're really rich.

So, lesson one, follow your feelings. If it feels right, move forward. If it doesn't feel right, don't do it.

Now I want to talk a little bit about failings, because nobody's journey is seamless or smooth. We all stumble. We all have setbacks. If things go wrong, you hit a dead end—as you will—it's just life's way of saying time to change course. So, ask every failure—this is what I do with every failure, every crisis, every difficult time—I say, what is this here to teach me? And as soon as you get the lesson, you get to move on. If you really get the lesson, you pass and you don't have to repeat the class. If you don't get the lesson, it shows up wearing another pair of pants—or skirt —to give you some remedial work.

And what I've found is that difficulties come when you don't pay attention to life's whisper, because life always whispers to you first. And if you ignore the whisper, sooner or later you'll get a scream. Whatever you resist persists. But, if you ask the right question—not why is this happening, but what is this here to teach me?—it puts you in the place and space to get the lesson you need.

My friend Eckhart Tolle, who's written this wonderful book called A New Earth that's all about letting the awareness of who you are stimulate everything that you do, he puts it like this: He says, don't react against a bad situation; merge with that situation instead. And the solution will arise from the challenge. Because surrendering yourself doesn't mean giving up; it means acting with responsibility.

Many of you know that, as President Hennessy said, I started this school in Africa. And I founded the school, where I'm trying to give South African girls a shot at a future like yours—Stanford. And I spent five years making sure that school would be as beautiful as the students. I wanted every girl to feel her worth reflected in her surroundings. So, I checked every blueprint, I picked every pillow. I was looking at the grout in between the bricks. I knew every thread count of the sheets. I chose every girl from the villages, from nine provinces. And yet, last fall, I was faced with a crisis I had never anticipated. I was told that one of the dorm matrons was suspected of sexual abuse.

That was, as you can imagine, devastating news. First, I cried—actually, I sobbed—for about half an hour. And then I said, let's get to it; that's all you get, a half an hour. You need to focus on the now, what you need to do now. So, I contacted a child trauma specialist. I put together a team of investigators. I made sure the girls had counseling and support. And Gayle and I got on a plane and flew to South Africa.

And the whole time I kept asking that question: What is this here to teach me? And, as difficult as that experience has been, I got a lot of lessons. I understand now the mistakes I made, because I had been paying attention to all of the wrong things. I'd built that school from the outside in, when what really mattered was the inside out.

So, it's a lesson that applies to all of our lives as a whole. What matters most is what's inside. What matters most is the sense of integrity, of quality and beauty. I got that lesson. And what I know is that the girls came away with something, too. They have emerged from this more resilient and knowing that their voices have power.

And their resilience and spirit have given me more than I could ever give to them, which leads me to my final lesson—the one about finding happiness—which we could talk about all day, but I know you have other wacky things to do.

Not a small topic this is, finding happiness. But in some ways I think it's the simplest of all. Gwendolyn Brooks wrote a poem for her children. It's called "Speech to the Young : Speech to the Progress-Toward." And she says at the end, "Live not for battles won. / Live not for the-end-of-the-song. / Live in the along." She's saying, like Eckhart Tolle, that you have to live for the present. You have to be in the moment. Whatever has happened to you in your past has no power over this present moment, because life is now.

But I think she's also saying, be a part of something. Don't live for yourself alone. This is what I know for sure: In order to be truly happy, you must live along with and you have to stand for something larger than yourself. Because life is a reciprocal exchange. To move forward you have to give back. And to me, that is the greatest lesson of life. To be happy, you have to give something back.

I know you know that, because that's a lesson that's woven into the very fabric of this university. It's a lesson that Jane and Leland Stanford got and one they've bequeathed to you. Because all of you know the story of how this great school came to be, how the Stanfords lost their only child to typhoid at the age of 15. They had every right and they had every reason to turn their backs against the world at that time, but instead, they channeled their grief and their pain into an act of grace. Within a year of their son's death, they had made the founding grant for this great school, pledging to do for other people's children what they were not able to do for their own boy.

The lesson here is clear, and that is, if you're hurting, you need to help somebody ease their hurt. If you're in pain, help somebody else's pain. And when you're in a mess, you get yourself out of the mess helping somebody out of theirs. And in the process, you get to become a member of what I call the greatest fellowship of all, the sorority of compassion and the fraternity of service.

The Stanfords had suffered the worst thing any mom and dad can ever endure, yet they understood that helping others is the way we help ourselves. And this wisdom is increasingly supported by scientific and sociological research. It's no longer just woo-woo soft-skills talk. There's actually a helper's high, a spiritual surge you gain from serving others. So, if you want to feel good, you have to go out and do some good.

But when you do good, I hope you strive for more than just the good feeling that service provides, because I know this for sure, that doing good actually makes you better. So, whatever field you choose, if you operate from the paradigm of service, I know your life will have more value and you will be happy.

I was always happy doing my talk show, but that happiness reached a depth of fulfillment, of joy, that I really can't describe to you or measure when I stopped just being on TV and looking at TV as a job and decided to use television, to use it and not have it use me, to use it as a platform to serve my viewers. That alone changed the trajectory of my success.

So, I know this—that whether you're an actor, you offer your talent in the way that most inspires art. If you're an anatomist, you look at your gift as knowledge and service to healing. Whether you've been called, as so many of you here today getting doctorates and other degrees, to the professions of business, law, engineering, humanities, science, medicine, if you choose to offer your skills and talent in service, when you choose the paradigm of service, looking at life through that paradigm, it turns everything you do from a job into a gift. And I know you haven't spent all this time at Stanford just to go out and get a job.

You've been enriched in countless ways. There's no better way to make your mark on the world and to share that abundance with others. My constant prayer for myself is to be used in service for the greater good.

So, let me end with one of my favorite quotes from Martin Luther King. Dr. King said, "Not everybody can be famous." And I don't know, but everybody today seems to want to be famous.

But fame is a trip. People follow you to the bathroom, listen to you pee. It's just—try to pee quietly. It doesn't matter, they come out and say, "Ohmigod, it's you. You peed."

That's the fame trip, so I don't know if you want that.

So, Dr. King said, "Not everybody can be famous. But everybody can be great, because greatness is determined by service." Those of you who are history scholars may know the rest of that passage. He said, "You don't have to have a college degree to serve. You don't have to make your subject and verb agree to serve. You don't have to know about Plato or Aristotle to serve. You don't have to know Einstein's theory of relativity to serve. You don't have to know the second theory of thermodynamics in physics to serve. You only need a heart full of grace and a soul generated by love."

In a few moments, you'll all be officially Stanford's '08.

You have the heart and the smarts to go with it. And it's up to you to decide, really, where will you now use those gifts? You've got the diploma, so go out and get the lessons, 'cause I know great things are sure to come.

You know, I've always believed that everything is better when you share it, so before I go, I wanted to share a graduation gift with you. Underneath your seats you'll find two of my favorite books. Eckhart Tolle's A New Earth is my current book club selection. Our *New Earth* webcast has been downloaded 30 million times with that book. And Daniel Pink's *A Whole New Mind: Why Right-Brainers Will Rule the Future* has reassured me I'm in the right direction.

I really wanted to give you cars but I just couldn't pull that off! Congratulations, '08!

Thank you. Thank you.

Key Words & Expressions

horsey *adjective* pertaining to, or characteristic of a horse.

on all fours of a person on the hands and feet, or the hands and knees: *They went on all fours to squeeze through the low opening.*

curfew *noun* a regulation requiring a person to be home at a certain prescribed time, as imposed by a parent on a child.

syndicate *verb* to sell a program, series, etc. directly to independent stations.

emulate *verb* to rival with some degree of success.

Barbara Walters an American journalist, writer, and media personality who has been a host on morning television shows (Today and The View), the evening news magazine 20/20), and co-anchor of ABC Evening News and correspondent on World News (then ABC Evening News). Walters was first known as a popular TV morning news anchor for over 10 years on NBC's Today.(http://www.wikipedia.org)

goofy *adjective* ridiculous, silly, wacky: *a goofy little doll.*

pileup *noun* a massive collision of several or many moving vehicles.

harness *verb* to bring under conditions for effective use: to harness wind power; *to harness the solar energy.*

matron *noun* a woman serving as a guard, warden, or attendant for women or girls, as in a prison.

resilience *noun* ability to recover readily from illness, depression, adversity.

typhoid *noun* Also called typhoid fever. an infectious, often fatal, febrile disease, usually of the summer months, characterized by intestinal inflammation and ulceration, caused by the typhoid bacillus, which is usually introduced with food or drink.

soft-skill *noun* a sociological term which refers to the cluster of personality traits, social graces, ability with language, personal habits, friendliness, and optimism that mark people to varying degrees: *Soft skills complement hard skills, which are the technical requirements of a job.*

Proverbs Related to the Text

- The world is like a school and our life is the classrooms.
- Feelings are really your GPS system for life.
- Don't react against a bad situation; merge with that situation instead.
- Not everybody can be famous. But everybody can be reat.

Listen and Fill in the Blanks.

I need to begin by ________ everyone ______ on a little secret. The secret is that Kirby Bumpus, Stanford Class of '08, is my ____________. So, I was _________ when President Hennessy asked me to be your Commencement speaker, because this is the first time _______ ________ allowed on campus since Kirby's ______ ______. You see, Kirby's a very smart girl. She wants people to get to know her ______ _______ _______ _______, she says. Not in terms of who she knows. So, she never wants anyone who's first meeting her to know that I know her and she knows me. So, when she first came to Stanford for new student orientation with her mom, I hear that they arrived and everybody was ____ _________, and somebody ______ ______ ______ Kirby and they said, "Ohmigod, that's Gayle King!" Because a lot of people know Gayle King as my BFF [best friend forever].
And so somebody comes up to Kirby, and they say, "Ohmigod, is that Gayle King?"
And Kirby's like, "Uh-huh. She's my mom."
And so the person says, "Ohmigod, does it mean, like, you know Oprah Winfrey?"

Pronunciation Bites

한국인 영어발음오류유형 14 : 문장 강세

TV나 영화 등의 원어민들이 말하는 것을 잘 들어보면 한 문장에서 한 단어, 엄밀히 말하면 한 음절이 유난히 두드러지게 크게 들린다는 것을 느낄 수 있다. 이것이 영어 문장의 특징 중의 하나이다. 이것은 단어 하나하나의 강세와는 별개의 문제로서 한 문장에서 특정 음절을 다른 음절과는 뚜렷한 구분을 두어 힘주어 발음함을 알 수 있다. 그러면 어떤 음절이 이러한 특권을 누리나? 다음 문장을 가지고 설명해 보자.

Martha bought a new comPUter.

특별한 경우가 아니면 이 문장은 마지막 단어인 computer의 단어강세위치인 두 번째 음절에 문장에서 제일 강한 강세가 오게 된다. 영어리듬의 또 다른 면이 이것이다. 이러한 발음상의 이유에서인지 영어에서는 가장 중요한 내용을 문장의 맨 뒤로 보내는 경향이 있다. 소위 '말미 초점 원칙'(principle of end focus)라는 것이다. 따라서 영어 문장을 들을 때는 문장의 마지막 단어까지 잘 들어야 한다. 정작 중요한 의미가 앞이 아닌 마지막에 있기 때문이다. 다만 다음과 같이 고유강세를 갖지 못하는 전치사, 대명사, 접속사 등은 문장 강세를 주지 않고 직전의 단어에 주어진다.

Benjamin bought a **new** one.

그러나 문장에서 특별한 의미, 예컨대 다른 대상과 대조, 또는 특정 단어를 강조하고 싶을 경우는 문장의 위치에 관계없이 강한 대조강세 (contrastive stress), 강조강세 (emphatic stress)를 줄 수 있다. 그러나 이 경우는 특별한 경우라는 점을 주의할 필요가 있다. 한국인들은 음절의존 리듬의 모국어답게 모든 단어를 동일한 강세를 주어 발음하는 경향이 있다. 억양 (intonation)의 변화폭도 중요하지만 강세의 정도의 변화를 주는 것도 영어의 리듬을 유지하는데 중요하다는 사실을 잊어서는 안 된다. 다음의 문장들을 발음해 보자.

Pronunciation Excercise

I've lost an umbrella.

Mike bought a new camera on Wednesday.

This plane goes to Atlanta.

She already finished them.

I've dropped him off.

Try it in English

1. 나는 3학점이 부족하다.

   I ________ three ________ __________.

2. 흠이 없는 사람은 없다.

   Nobody is __________.

3. 그 사람은 세상에 등을 돌렸다.

   He ________ ________ ________ against the world.

For Improvement of Your Critical Thinking

Question: Oprah Winfrey concluded her long speech by saying "every thing is better when you share it." Have you ever given service to others without payment? Have you ever thought about it? Describe what you have done or thought about.

Oprah Winfrey

The Oprah Winfrey Show (often simply referred to as *Oprah* or simply just *O*) is a United States syndicated talk show, hosted and produced by its namesake Oprah Winfrey, and is the highest-rated talk show in American television history. It is currently the longest-running daytime television talk show in the United States, having run nationally since September 8, 1986, for over 22 seasons and 3,000 episodes (as of September 10, 2007). The show is renewed through 2011, but in a 2007 interview with Larry King, Oprah said that in 2011, she will not renew her contract, thus ending the show. The show, a production of Harpo Productions, is the last program currently on the air to be distributed by King World (only the name is mentioned in the Friday show's distribution credits), even though the latter company has been absorbed by CBS Television Distribution.

Oprah has been included in Time magazine's shortlist of the best television series of the twentieth century in 1998, and it made the top 50 of *TV Guide*'s countdown of the greatest American shows of all time in 2002.

The show is highly influential, especially with women,[citation needed] and many of its topics penetrate into American pop-cultural consciousness. While early episodes of the show followed a Phil Donahue-style exploration of sensationalistic social issues, Oprah eventually transformed her series into a more positive, spiritually uplifting experience marked by book clubs, celebrity interviews, self-improvement segments, and philanthropic forays into world events.

(http://www.wikipedia.org)

Whole Language Approach
Internet-Aided English Learning 2

Snap Shots of Heroes of our Mind

First Published May 2010
SHINASA Publishing Co.
28-36 NokBeon-Dong, EunPyung-Gu, Seoul, Korea
Registered : 9-52 (Jan. 5 1956)
Tel : 02-382-6411
Fax : 02-382-6401
E-mail : shinasa@chol.com / Homepage : www.shinasa.co.kr
ISBN : 978-89-8396-671-1
Printed and bounded in Korea

₩ 10,000